P9-DFT-752

Dear Reader:

The book you are about to read is the latest bestseller from the St. Martin's True Crime Library, the imprint the *New York Times* calls "the leader in true crime!" Each month, we offer you a fascinating account of the latest, most sensational crime that has captured the national attention. St. Martin's is the publisher of perennial bestselling true crime author Jack Olsen whose SALT OF THE EARTH is the true story of one woman's triumph over life-shattering violence; Joseph Wambaugh called it "powerful and absorbing." Fannie Weinstein and Melinda Wilson tell the story of a beautiful honors student who was lured into the dark world of sex for hire in THE COED CALL GIRL MURDER. St. Martin's is also proud to publish critically acclaimed author Carlton Stowers, whose 1999 Edgar Award-winning TO THE LAST BREATH recounts a two-year-old girl's mysterious death, and the dogged investigation that led loved ones to the most unlikely murderer: her own father. In the book you now hold, BLIND PASSION, a romance between a beautiful model and a charming sailor leads to a tragic outcome.

St. Martin's True Crime Library gives you the stories *behind* the headlines. Our authors take you right to the scene of the crime and into the minds of the most notorious murderers to show you what really makes them tick. St. Martin's True Crime Library paperbacks are better than the most terrifying thriller, because it's all true! The next time you want a crackling good read, make sure it's got the St. Martin's True Crime Library logo on the spine—you'll be up all night!

Charles E. Spicer, Jr.
Executive Editor, St. Martin's True Crime Library

They fell into silence again as Skiadopoulos slowed down the car, his steely eyes searching the rows upon rows of vineyards stretching off into the distance. It was a lonely stretch of road that his father used to take him to as a boy. No one ever came here in the winter, especially on a rainy night like this. It was the perfect place to carry out his dark enterprise.

He finally saw a suitable opening and turned into it, telling Julie that he had to relieve himself. She felt an icy shiver run down her neck as she saw the desolate swamp loom up ahead in the bright headlights of the Fiat.

Skiadopoulos stopped the car and turned off the engine and slowly turned towards Julie in the passenger seat, summoning up his courage. There was a strange look on his face that Julie had never seen before, and it scared her . . .

BLIND PASSION

A TRUE STORY OF SEDUCTION, OBSESSION AND MURDER

JOHN GLATT

St. Martin's Paperbacks

NOTE: If you purchased this book without a cover you should be aware that this book is stolen property. It was reported as "unsold and destroyed" to the publisher, and neither the author nor the publisher has received any payment for this "stripped book."

BLIND PASSION

Copyright © 2000 by John Glatt.

Cover photograph of Julie Scully courtesy AP/Wide World Photos. Photograph of ocean courtesy PhotoDisc.

All rights reserved. No part of this book may be used or reproduced in any manner whatsoever without written permission except in the case of brief quotations embodied in critical articles or reviews. For information address St. Martin's Press, 175 Fifth Avenue, New York, N.Y. 10010.

ISBN: 0-312-97559-7

Printed in the United States of America

St. Martin's Paperbacks edition / July 2000

10 9 8 7 6 5 4 3 2 1

For Susan Elizabeth Chenery

ACKNOWLEDGMENTS

In many ways the sad story of Julie Scully represents the dark side of the American dream. The all-American girl who grew up to be a beautiful model apparently had the world at her feet. But she threw it all away in a desperate search for love with a dangerously troubled Greek stranger whom she met while cruising the Caribbean with her husband.

I first read about Julie's horrific murder in London, England, and decided to discover what had set her on her path to destruction. At first sight so many aspects of Julie's savage killing did not make sense. I was intrigued by why had she abandoned everything to move to a desolate part of northern Greece, in pursuit of an unrealistic dream.

After enlisting the support of Julie's ex-husband, Tim Nist, and that of her family, I immersed myself in Julie's life for a year, trying to unravel the mystery that surrounds her death. Spending time in Kavala, Greece, I visited the places where her lover George Skiadopoulos had grown up and where Julie would die so violently at his hands.

I am deeply indebted to Julie's friends and family, who all fully cooperated with this book. Most of all I would like to thank Tim Nist for his patience and candor during our many hours of conversation at his house. Few husbands have had to endure the trials he has and there were many emotional moments as he relived his seven-year marriage to Julie.

Much gratitude is also owed to Julie's mother, Julia Scully, who has suffered horribly since her daughter's murder. In our often tearful talks she remained objective as she willingly discussed her beloved daughter.

Thanks must also go to Julie's father, John Scully Sr., and her brother, John Scully Jr., for the kindness in sharing details of Julie's childhood and early life.

I also spent many hours talking to many of Julie's friends, who were all hit hard by her untimely death. Her best friend Tracey Allen was a constant source of inspiration for me as I wrote the book and I am also indebted to Susan White and Cheryl Chuplis for their remembrance of Julie. In particular Tony Capella provided a clear, objective view of Julie's final years and her decline.

I am also indebted to Athen's AP Bureau's Brian and Tula Murphy, Patrick Quinn and my wonderful translator Theodora Tongas, who helped pave the way during my stay in Greece. I would also like to thank George Frimis of Antenna TV and the Dean of Greek Crime Reporters, Panos Somboulos, both of whom provided invaluable background on the case. I also spent an interesting two hours with George Skiadopoulos's attorney, Sakis Kehagioglou, at his office in Athens.

In Kavala I was greatly helped by local journalist Vasilicki Liotaki who showed me the town, introducing me to Skiadopoulos's friends, Demetrios Copsahelios and Alexis Makezedis.

In Philadelphia I was greatly helped by Vince Ziemba, Kenneth Freeman, and Judge Paul Panepinto of Philadelphia Family Court.

Thanks also goes to *The Trentonian* newspaper which kindly gave me access to its files. Especially helpful was Eric Ladley, city editor Paul Micole, and publisher Dave Bonfield. I am also indebted to Tom Kelly, Cyndi Manion, Sandy Schwartz and Liberty of the Greek Press Office in New York as well as the many others I interviewed who wished to remain anonymous.

But one of my biggest debts of gratitude must go to my editor at St. Martin's Press, Charles Spicer, for his encouragement. Credit is also due to my literary agent lion, Peter Miller and his staff and PMA.

My thanks also to: Joseph Cleeman, Annette Witheridge, Danny Trachtenberg, Cari Pokrassa, Chris Bowen, Roger Hitts, Fred and Linda Wehner, Chris Wilson, Wensley Clarkson, Katie Lyons, Daphna Inbar, Scott Flander, Earl Wallace and Bobby Fisher.

CONTENTS

"Today, tomorrow and forever
you are going to be my love"

George Skiadopoulos, July 7, 1998

PROLOGUE

As his theme music begins, popular talk-show host Maury Povich introduces the second of his two subjects for this afternoon's program. After a series of triple split-screen shots of the silver-haired host in action, the camera zooms in slowly toward the stage to an enthusiastic burst of audience applause. There, clapping her long slender hands, sits a stunningly beautiful dark-haired young woman, wearing just the briefest of bikinis. On either side of her are two conservatively dressed older women and to their left, a smug-looking man with a mustache, meticulously dressed with the sort of brightly colored tie that dazzles television screens.

Standing behind them in a semi-circle are fifteen other shapely bikini-clad women. But they almost pale into insignificance next to the stunningly beautiful girl in front, who has obviously been singled out for special attention.

Another camera pans in from the stage toward Maury

Povich, who now waves a copy of a brightly colored tabloid newspaper at the audience.

"Today, what's being called sleazy, a slutty journalism that we don't want," he begins, brandishing the newspaper with the headline LEAVE MY TURNPIKE PALS. ALONE, at the camera.

Informing the audience that the Pulitzer Prize-winning New Jersey *Trentonian* has recently boosted its circulation dramatically with pictures of "near-naked women" right alongside the news, Povich also notes that thousands of readers have canceled their subscriptions in protest.

Moving to "B" roll, a middle-aged photographer named Tom Kelly is seen gently coaxing the same dark-haired girl in the front row into a provocative pose outside the State Capitol in Trenton. Wearing an even skimpier bikini, she seductively hugs a wide stone column as a party of schoolchildren walk by.

"Come on, Julie, smile, all right," he says, unleashing a barrage of shots as she smiles radiantly into his Nikon lens.

It is the summer of 1992 and *The Trentonian*'s innovative marketing gimmick to use glamour to sell newspapers has stirred up a hornet's nest in the city and its strait-laced suburbs. Although the idea is nothing new—in England the Rupert Murdoch-owned tabloid *The Sun* has had far racier pictures of topless models on its Page 3 for nearly a quarter of a century—it has plunged *The Trentonian* into national controversy.

Each day a local girl in a sexy bikini is featured on *The Trentonian*'s Page 6, people page, and each month they compete for a $1,000 prize and a place in the paper's annual swimsuit calendar. In the two years since the Page 6 girls were introduced, circulation has jumped ten percent and turned some of the girls into local celebrities.

The best-known Page 6 girl by far is twenty-four-year-old Julie Nist, who is here to defend *The Trentonian* against its critics on national television. Julie has appeared on Page 6 ten times in two years, and has twice been voted its swimsuit model of the year.

Her exotic looks are inherited from her full-blooded Navajo mother. Long dark hair frames her perfect almond-shaped brown eyes set between impossibly high cheek-bones. And her beauty and charisma have already propelled her off Page 6 to a successful modeling career.

Julie Nist is a far cry from the public perception of a stereotyped bimbo. A highly articulate straight-A student, *Trentonian* editor Gale Baldwin asked her to appear on the show only the night before to help him defend the paper against its detractors, of which there are many.

Indeed, even the genial, craggy-faced Povich, who for years anchored America's pioneering tabloid television show *A Current Affair*, appears censorious toward *The Trentonian*. But the paper's editor is totally unrepentant, brushing off his critics as "hypocritical, pompous asses."

Sitting to the right of Julie Nist is the president of the National Association of Women's New Jersey chapter, Donna Puluka. A stern-looking woman in her mid-thirties, Puluka is modestly attired in a dark gray suit and floral silk scarf. And she passionately believes that the Page 6 girl insults all women and debases them.

Julie, who would later admit to being nervous at the prospect of facing Puluka, had had only hours to prepare her defense of *The Trentonian* on national television. The previous night she had lain in bed carefully rehearsing her arguments with her new husband Tim, who is in the audience. "I racked my brain for an angle to take," she would later say.

From the beginning Puluka goes on the offensive, accusing the paper of using women as sales objects and not having enough journalistic merits to survive without them.

"It's fun," laughs Julie, as the camera pans in for a close-up of her perfect face. "People enjoy it—men and women alike."

Asked by Povich why she has already appeared in *The Trentonian* ten times, Julie replies it definitely sells newspapers and as a professional model she has no problem showing off her body.

Turning to the audience, Povich asks what it thinks of Julie's glamour photo session on the steps of the State Capitol, in full view of elementary-school pupils. Suddenly a very tall, athletic-looking man in his early thirties rises from his seat with a smirk on his face.

"It's not that it happens all the time," he laughs, explaining that Julie is his wife.

As Povich starts walking away, Tim Nist cockily grabs him by the shoulder, hauling him back as Julie proudly applauds her husband's antics. But an unamused Povich tells Tim that he does not wish to talk to him.

Without missing a beat, Tim Nist suddenly asks Povich if his own wife, Connie Chung, really got to anchor the *CBS Evening News* with Dan Rather on journalistic skills alone.

Povich's eyes flash with anger as he defends his wife against Tim's cheeky accusation that Chung's looks helped her career. Then he goes straight into a commercial.

As part two begins, Povich goes on the offensive

against *The Trentonian*, asking if the Page 6 model's poses are exploitative and seductive.

"I don't feel so," replies Julie. "If I may, I'll *show* you poses."

Then to the astonishment of Povich and the audience, Julie rises from her seat as several audience members gasp in astonishment."

Delighted to be able to perform, Julie sits down on the front of the stage and strikes a series of sexy, uninhibited poses for the camera.

"We only do something like this," she says innocently. "Does *that* offend anyone?"

"OK, thank you Julie," admonishes Povich. "You can get back up in your chair."

Later Julie would describe her appearance on the show as triumphant and *the* defining moment of her life.

On a beautiful Sunday morning five years later, Julie Nist is sunbathing on a beach with her friend Tony Capella. It is still early but already the sun is beating down on a deserted stretch of sand in front of the vacation house Tim Nist has rented on Long Beach island.

A close friend of the Nists', and godfather of their twenty-one-month-old daughter Katie Scarlett, Tony is a confidant of Julie's and has become increasingly concerned about her welfare. It is his suggestion that they go to the beach and talk, leaving Tim inside with Katie.

Since her appearance on *The Maury Povich Show*, the former swimsuit model is scarcely recognizable. Having gained more than thirty pounds since the birth of her daughter, Julie's once-perfect body is no longer in demand for modeling.

Initially she had loved being a mother, throwing herself into it with the same gusto she had once reserved for modeling. But now, as she approaches her thirtieth birthday, Julie has become clinically depressed and is seeing a psychiatrist, who has put her on Prozac and anti-depressants.

Still more worrying for Capella is Julie's heavy drinking and increasing use of cocaine.

"I'll never forget," says Capella. "Out of the blue she turned to me and says, 'You know, I don't think I deserve my life.' "

"I looked at her and said, 'That's crazy. Why would you not think you deserve the life you have?' "

To the outside world Julie Nist seems to have it all. A rich, loving husband, a beautiful little girl, and enough money to live in luxury, buying expensive jewelry, fast cars and anything else that takes her fancy. She lives in a chic two-story Colonial in an exclusive part of Southern New Jersey, usually taking two or three foreign vacations every year.

But in the last few months, Julie has become despondent, her bubbly spirit sinking to an all-time low. She has grown morose, seldom venturing out of bed during the day and complaining that she is constantly tired.

The only time she seems happy is when she goes out partying with friends. Then she gets drunk and takes drugs, never quite knowing when to stop.

Her six-year marriage to Tim is breaking up. The couple have recently gone into counseling to try and save it. But they both know it is only a matter of time before they split.

When a sympathetic Capella pushes her to explain why she doesn't think she deserves her life, Julie refuses to elaborate. On reflection he would conclude that she was using the conversation to talk herself out of some dangerous new course of action she is already contemplating.

"That was when she stopped being herself anymore," remembers Capella. "Because up to then everything seemed wonderful for her and Tim. She was a good person, a good mother. Looking back I can see that something had really gone wrong. She was already set on the path to destruction."

A few months later, in a desperate search for love and excitement, Julie would abandon everything in search of an impossible dream. She would leave her daughter to run off to Greece with a young sailor named George Skiadopoulos, whom she'd meet on a cruise. And when their passionate romance would burn itself out and become a nightmare, Skiadopoulos would never allow her to return to America alive.

PART ONE

JULIE

CHAPTER ONE

NAVAJO ROOTS

From her earliest childhood, Julie Nist was aware of her Navajo heritage and that she was special. As a young child she talked to animals and always had a deep, instinctual love of nature that would remain until the end of her life.

While her father, John Scully, a north Philadelphia beat cop, worked nights, her mother, Julia, would tell her children stories about their tribal roots and heritage. Each night Julia would recite the same Navajo folklore she had learned from her mother growing up on the Four Corners Reservation in New Mexico; magical stories that had been passed down through the generations.

One special favorite of Julie and her little brother was the legend of the good witch Spider Woman. When the ancient Navajo stepped out of the third World into our present fourth one, Spider Woman, who possessed strange, supernatural powers, used her magic to help them fight evil monsters.

Julie and John loved to hear how Spider Woman gave special powers to Monster-Slayer and his sister Child-Born-of-Water, to help them in their quest to find their long-lost father, Sun-God. Then when the family was triumphantly reunited, Sun-God showed his children how to destroy all the evil monsters forever, so the Navajo could live in peace and harmony.

Unfortunately Julia and her daughter would never be able to quell their own demons and find peace.

Julia Scully was born in Twin Lakes on February 12, 1943, the youngest child of Miriam and Sam Bowman. She grew up with her three brothers and two sisters in the spectacular red-rock, deep-canyoned New Mexico side of the twenty-four-thousand-square-mile reservation, bordering the states of Utah, Colorado and Arizona.

The two-hundred-thousand-strong Navajo people is the largest Indian nation in the United States and had suffered greatly since the Spanish first colonized their lands in the 15th century. It was a tortured history drenched in blood, leaving an indelible mark on each member of the tribe to this day.

The white invaders introduced sheep and horses to the Navajo, who soon used the animals for their nomadic way of life. They became excellent horsemen and began raiding the Spanish settlements in revenge.

But once the United States defeated Spain and assumed control of the vast tribal lands, the army used extreme brutality to tame the Navajo. It was a dark time for the Navajo nation as they were systematically robbed of their lands by the legendary Kit Carson, who burned their villages, slaughtering hundreds of men, women and children.

By 1864 most of the Navajo nation had been defeated

and the United States government decided to forcibly move the tribe from the Four Sacred Mountains to Fort Sumner, three hundred miles east. During what has become known as the "Long Walk," more than two hundred Navajos perished from starvation and the inhuman conditions they encountered during their compulsory exodus through the burning desert.

The survivors were imprisoned in Fort Sumner, where they were herded into the barren land, which was unable to support their cattle and crops. Any Navajo who tried to escape back to their homeland were hunted down and ruthlessly killed by the army.

After four torturous years, which saw hundreds of Navajo die from starvation, the Federal Government signed a new treaty in 1868. This allowed the tribe to return to their beloved Four Sacred Mountains, where they remain to this day. For the last one hundred and thirty years the proud tribe has eked out a living, raising sheep and selling its unique crafts, including rugs, jewelry and silverwork.

Julia's father Sam Bowman was born in 1895 on the reservation near Shiprock, New Mexico. He had married and had four children before his wife died as a young woman.

In the early 1930s during a visit to Twin Lakes, New Mexico, Sam met a beautiful young woman named Miriam, who was fifteen years younger than him. They soon fell in love and after marrying in a traditional ceremony, Sam remained in Twin Lakes to live near Miriam's family.

Sam began raising goats and sheep to support his new wife, who used the wool to weave intricate rugs in the traditional Navajo style for sale to tourists. During the summer they grew fruit and vegetables, and were self-sufficient. Sam Bowman's entire family, consisting of grandparents, aunts, uncles and cousins all lived in the same village in traditional Navajo houses, called hogans, within a few yards of each other.

Over the years, Sam and Miriam had six children and it was often a struggle to survive, but the children never went hungry and were always well-clothed. Times were hard as the twentieth-century Navajos slowly assimilated into the American system, still retaining their ancient traditions and way of life.

There were few jobs on the reservation and Sam Bowman's cattle business was highly precarious, given frequent droughts and extremes in temperatures. The long summers were brutally hot, bringing dust storms, and in the winter the temperatures plunged to freezing and often brought snow.

To protect his family and his cattle, Sam and his brother used their own hands to dig a simple shelter in a nearby hill to protect them from the cold. One of Julia's earliest memories is of lying in the dug-out with the cattle to keep warm on the long winter nights, listening to her mother's stories of the ancient Navajo folklore.

"But in the summertime, no matter how hot it was, it was always cool in there," remembers Julia.

Life was tough on the reservation in the 1950s with no electricity or running water. Alcoholism was a major problem as more and more Navajo turned to drink in order to escape the growing pressures of modern life. The environment Julia grew up in, and her father's strict discipline, would have a lasting effect on the young girl after she made her own way in the world.

When she was twelve, Julia, who spoke fluent Navajo, was sent away to an Indian boarding school in

Brigham City, Utah, to learn to read and write in English.

"I hadn't realized that there was a world outside," says Julia. "It was the first time I had ever left the reservation."

Always headstrong and independent, the pretty, dark-haired Julia hated the rules and restrictions that were imposed on her. And after a couple of years at the boarding school, she told her parents she wasn't going back.

Sam and Miriam were sympathetic and arranged for her to go to another boarding school for American Indian children near Carson City, Nevada. But the adventurous girl longed to see more of the world outside the reservation.

So when she was sixteen, she took a three-month summer job in Sacramento, California, caring for two little boys as a mother's helper. When her new employers flew to New York to celebrate their wedding anniversary, Julia took the boys to stay with their grandparents in San Francisco.

It was the first time Julia had ever been in a big city, with its modern skyscrapers and frenetic way of life. She found it a revelation and, with a mixture of excitement and fear, timidly explored her new surroundings, resolving to leave the reservation at the earliest possible opportunity.

"They lived on the seventeenth floor," she recalls, "and they had a patio but I was so scared I wouldn't even go out."

Every day, when the boys were napping, Julia timidly ventured out of the building to walk to the street corner. There she would stand entranced for hours, watching the non-stop stream of traffic and pedestrians, dreaming of living in such a wondrous place where anything seemed possible.

The following year she took another summer job caring for a rich couple's children in the desert oasis of Lake Tahoe in Nevada. It was another life-changing experience for the teenager, who loved the excitement of the gambling mecca, even though she never set foot inside a casino.

When Julia graduated from school, she told her parents she would not be returning to the reservation. Her mother was very concerned for her youngest daughter, knowing the prejudice that she would encounter in the outside world. Besides, no one else in their family had ever wanted to leave the reservation before.

"I guess I was the only one who wanted to go and see other things," said Julia. "There was nothing really to keep me on the reservation. But my mother said it would be all right as long as I was happy."

In 1961, at the age of eighteen, Julia Bowman moved to Reno, Nevada, with stars in her eyes. She soon found a job as a hospital aide and began finding her feet. At first she made frequent trips home to visit her parents but she never stayed long, itching to return to her exciting new life in the glamourous casino town.

Two years later Sam Bowman was diagnosed with diabetes and Julia dutifully went back to Twin Lakes to help care for him. But the following spring she left again, this time heading east to Colorado Springs, where she found a job as a dietary assistant in a private hospital for the mentally ill.

Every Tuesday some of the patients would receive electroconvulsive therapy. As part of her job, Julia prepared their special diet trays for when they came out of the treatment. It was a terrible ordeal for the sensitive young girl to witness the misery of the patients first-hand, as she fed them.

It was here that Julia was first introduced to amphetamines by a female friend at the hospital. One day at a friend's apartment she was given a glass of iced tea which had been laced with speed. Before long Julia was addicted to amphetamines.

"The thing with the pills was that I could stay up for forty-eight hours," she said. "But although I would become really irritable, I always wanted to do them."

Her friend had a prescription for the diet pills with no restrictions for refills, so Julia went to the drug store to buy supplies. She found speed helped her get through her tough job as well as to stay up late.

There was an active social scene among the hospital staff she met in the canteen. A couple of times a week she would join her new friends for a night out in the lively bars in Colorado Springs, where they drank heavily. And the friendly, attractive Indian girl proved very popular and was often asked out on dates.

On July 4, 1964, she was celebrating Independence Day in a bar when she was introduced to a tall, handsome military policeman named John Scully, who was stationed at nearby Fort Carson on a two-year round of service.

Born in Philadelphia, Scully was twenty-five years old and his background was worlds apart from Julia's. A soft-spoken conservative young man enjoying his stint out West in the military, he didn't appear to have much in common with the full-blooded Navajo girl, but John was captivated by her dark exotic beauty and there was an immediate physical attraction between them.

They got off to a bad start when Scully told her they

had met a few weeks earlier when he was dating one of her friends, and Julia couldn't remember. But after breaking the ice, he asked her out the following Saturday, she agreed. Within a week they were courting.

However, the relationship had to be put on hold when John had to go back to Philadelphia for a couple of months. Upon his return he immediately telephoned Julia and on one of their first dates surprised her by proposing marriage. She agreed.

"I was just a kid," said Julia. "We were at a party when he suddenly announced he always knew we would be married. It had never even occurred to me."

A couple of weeks later Julia returned to the reservation with the news of her engagement. Her parents were concerned that it was too soon for her to marry but reluctantly gave their blessing, saying they were happy if this was what she wanted.

John and Julia were married in a simple Catholic ceremony in Colorado Springs on July 2, 1965. They moved into a small apartment but were too poor to go on a proper honeymoon.

Soon after they were married John completed his military service and found a construction job. But just after Labor Day he told his new wife that they were moving east, across the country to Philadelphia. He explained that the seasonal construction work in Colorado Springs had come to an end, and there were far more job opportunities to pursue in Philadelphia.

Julia feared such a big move and being two thousand miles away from her family, but John assured her that if she was not happy they would move back again.

"I didn't have any choice," says Julia. "He knew exactly what he wanted so I finally said OK."

Julia insisted that John first come back to Twin Lakes

to meet her family and spend a few days on the reservation. It would be five years before Julia went home again, and the last time she would ever see her father alive.

John and Julia Scully arrived in Philadelphia in the midst of one of the coldest winters on record. They moved into a small row house in the staunchly working-class north Philadelphia suburb of Kensington, also known as Fishtown. Once the textile capital of the United States, Kensington was now a drab, gray place littered with mills and factories, spewing thick black smoke high into the air. It was a long way away from the scenic wide-open spaces Julia had grown up in. She found it very hard to adapt and missed her family terribly.

"I didn't know anyone except my husband," she remembers. "It was very hard and I was homesick."

In the close-knit neighborhood where everyone knew one another, the pretty Navajo girl stood out and was often mistaken for Filipino or Korean. Although the neighbors were friendly enough to her face, Julia always felt she was being looked down upon.

They settled down on the same street as John Scully's parents, just two blocks away from John's twin brother Joseph. Julia did her best to make a good impression when she was first introduced to his family, but it would take many months before she was accepted.

Soon after they arrived John applied to join the Philadelphia Police Department. While he was waiting for the results his brother Joseph found him a job in a refrigeration plant. Julia also found a job in a shoe factory, doing menial piece work to supplement their income.

John was delighted when he heard that he had passed the application test. On February 6, 1966, he officially joined the Philadelphia Police Department as a beat cop in the tough Seventh Precinct on Bustleton and Bower Street in north Philadelphia. Although the job paid well, his shifts alternated between days and nights. It was tough on Julia, who found herself alone at home most nights, and she became even more homesick.

But everything changed in the spring of 1967 when she found out she was pregnant. Julia was delighted at the prospect of a baby, believing it would give her a new purpose in life. Now she would have company to occupy her time. She began preparing for motherhood by buying baby clothes, while John set up a nursery in an upstairs room.

Finally Julia was beginning to settle down in Philadelphia and seemed to be happy and content. But it was a rare period of peace in the Scullys' marriage, which would soon burst apart at the seams with terrible consequences.

CHAPTER TWO

FAMILY TROUBLE

Julie Marie Scully was born on January 3, 1968, weighing six pounds, seven ounces. She was a beautiful baby with a warm, enticing smile that made everyone want to pick her up and hug her. Photogenic from the very beginning, the chubby little baby was a picture of happiness, languidly stretched out in her cot with a single tuft of dark hair jutting out of her round head.

Photographs of her christening show the angelic baby almost lost in a massive white lacy dress, as she is held aloft by her proud parents.

"By the time she was three months she was sitting up," remembers her mother. "She always wanted to learn and she was faster than the other kids."

Soon after Julie's birth her father bought a trailer in Dennisville Lake Campground in southern New Jersey, so the family could escape to the country for long weekends. The adventurous black-haired toddler loved nature, and would spend hours exploring the beautiful countryside and lake with her father. Later she would remember her trips to Dennisville Lake as the happiest time of her life.

"I had her out there crabbing with me from the very beginning," said John Scully, who was delighted to discover that his daughter shared his love of fishing. "By the time Julie was three she could pick up a crab without it biting her. And I don't believe she's ever been bitten by a crab."

It was during these weekend trips that Julie closely bonded with her father, through their common love of fishing and nature. As a young child Julie always sought her father's approval, knowing she could expect a big hug whenever she caught a crab. But while father and daughter happily amused themselves for hours, Julia felt left out and bored. She usually sat by herself outside the trailer, longing to go home.

Throughout their marriage Julia had been secretly addicted to speed and now it was catching up with her, making her moody and erratic. One day, when Julie was five months old, her mother was walking along Front Street with a friend when she suddenly fainted.

"It scared the hell out of me," said Julia. "I went to the doctor and he gave me more diet pills because of my blood pressure and the fainting spells. Now I was on them all the time and when I went back he discovered that my system needed them."

The doctor persuaded the young mother to cut back on amphetamines, slowly weaning her off them. She managed to kick her habit for a couple of years but she missed the way the pills had made her feel. For the next few years Julia would have a major problem with drug addiction.

On November 10, 1969, Julia gave birth to a healthy

baby boy named John Patrick Scully, to the delight of his father. John Scully Senior would always be far closer to his son than to Julie, who loved him dearly and continually sought his love and affection.

Soon after John Junior was born the family moved into a bigger house around the corner on North Palethorp Street. Julia quit her job to become a full-time mother but her husband worked harder than ever. From that time on he was hardly ever at home with his family. Every week he alternated working days and nights and his frequent absences disrupted family life. Even at Christmas, John Scully was rarely around to celebrate with his children, and Julia found herself single-handedly bringing them up.

"That was the hardest part," Julia remembered. "I had to do everything myself because he was never there."

When Julie was three, her mother took the children back to New Mexico to stay on the reservation and meet her Navajo relatives. It had been the first time Julia had been back since her father Sam Bowman had died a couple of years earlier.

"Julie loved being there," remembers Julia. "I had told her all kinds of stuff about the Navajo and we had a great time."

Although they stayed with Julia's mother, the adventurous little girl was mostly at her Aunt Mary's home playing with her three elder cousins, who made a big fuss over her and taught her to ride horses. It would be the beginning of a life-long friendship with her American Indian cousins.

Soon after they returned to Philadelphia, Julie was out with her mother when she suddenly dashed out into a one-way street and was hit by a speeding motorbike. The little girl was rushed to the hospital with serious internal injuries. Surgeons removed her spleen in an emergency operation to save her life, leaving a clearly visible scar on her stomach.

During her slow and painful recovery, Julie astonished her doctors by her bravery. While the other children in the ward howled and screamed about taking their medicine, little Julie almost seemed to welcome it. She even appeared to enjoy the pain-killing drugs she was injected with, alarming her mother. After her own experience with drugs, Julia worried that her daughter would come to associate a needle with euphoria and falling asleep.

Less than a week after the accident Julie left the hospital and her mother enrolled her in a local kindergarten to keep her out of harm's way. She also started taking the children camping at Dennisville Lake as often as possible, feeling that the countryside was far safer than the dangerous streets of Kensington.

In 1973 Julia decided to kick speed once and for all. The drug was now making her lose her temper at the slightest provocation. She found a sympathetic doctor who told her it would be too dangerous to go "cold turkey" as she had a serious dependency. He gradually weaned her off amphetamines by giving her smaller and smaller doses, until she stopped altogether. Julia was only too well aware that the drugs were now endangering her marriage, and successfully stopped using them for a time.

Now clean, Julia found herself unable to face the responsibilities of bringing up two children with an ever-absent husband.

"Everything had changed," she remembered. "He wasn't the same person as he used to be and could be cruel. When my children were little we didn't have a family life like our neighbors. Either he was working or he was going to work."

Now Julia fell into a deep depression, feeling trapped in Kensington with no one to talk to about her marital problems. She couldn't sleep at night and rarely got out of bed during the day. Finally, one night she could not take it anymore and tried to kill herself, by taking an overdose of sleeping pills that she had been collecting.

"I was *so* depressed," she recalled. "John was working that night and I put the kids to bed. When he came home at 11:30 p.m. he found me [unconscious] and took me to Friends Hospital where they pumped my stomach."

While in the hospital she told a psychiatrist about her problems at home and her chronic insomnia. He prescribed tranquilizers to calm her down.

"They relaxed me and I got better," she explained. "I still take the pills to this day."

But after being discharged and returning home, Julia's substance abuse problems would become even worse, making her own children reject her.

Ironically, it was her husband who first encouraged Julia to drink socially. In the past she had always forgone alcohol as it gave her bad hangovers and made her feel ill. But one night John Senior was extolling the virtues of peach brandy, so she tried one and liked it.

"I guess I never really knew how to drink," she said. "I didn't like beer as I thought it had a nasty taste, but we always had a lot of the stuff at home. In the end I began drinking it."

While on beat patrol in Northeast Philadelphia, Scully would often confiscate beer from underage drinkers. He would then take it home and store it in the refrigerator in the kitchen.

At first Julia drank to relieve the boredom of the long hours she spent alone, after putting the children to bed. But she quickly became addicted and was soon drinking so much beer, and bingeing on food, that her slender five-foot, one-inch body ballooned from one hundred and twelve pounds to one hundred and ninety pounds.

Years later she would be told by a counselor that American Indians have no resistance to alcohol because they don't have the necessary enzymes to process it properly.

"We can't stop," she said. "I guess I acquired a taste for beer."

Her escalating weight problems were compounded by the tranquilizers and sleeping pills she was also taking, which made her constantly crave food. She no longer bothered to make the children sit down at the dinner table for meals after they returned home from St. Boniface Elementary School, which they now both attended.

Julia would start drinking early and then leave their meals out for them to eat whenever they felt like it. John Scully now only came home to sleep and Julia says she hardly ever saw him.

The busy policeman seemed to have little time or patience for John and Julie. At Christmas he would take them to a toy store and wait outside while they went in to choose their own presents. The two Scully children felt deprived of the love and attention they saw friends receive from their parents.

As she piled on weight, Julia became even more depressed and had little self-esteem. She took another overdose and had to be rushed to the hospital by her husband to have her stomach pumped again.

But this time when she returned home things took a violent turn, as she began to beat Julie and her little brother John in an alcoholic haze.

"She hit Julie and me at times very hard and very often," says John Junior. "Sometimes with her hands and sometimes with whatever was available. It was not a normal childhood."

With their mother often out of the house, the children were left alone for long periods. Julie would take care of her younger brother, who was far less secure than she was. In time she became a kind of surrogate mother to the needy young boy.

"Julie took care of me," remembered John. "I know my mom loved Julie and me but it wasn't pleasant."

Although the children complained about the beatings to their father, he did little to prevent them. Today he claims that he learned about the violence much later, but he says he never witnessed it first-hand.

"I recall Julie telling me that her mother used to grab her by the hair and pull her around the house," he said.

Today Julia Scully readily admits beating her children, but denies it had anything to do with her own upbringing.

"People assumed I got this way because of [my parents]," she said. "I said no. It was because I got fat from drinking beer."

She claims that her husband was also cruel toward the children, citing one occasion when the family was camping at Dennisville Lake and little John accidentally "messed his pants." Furious at his son, John Senior smacked his bottom to teach him a lesson, causing the sensitive little boy to become chronically constipated. "For a long time John had problems," said his mother.

"He wouldn't go [to the bathroom]. He would just hold it in."

In their formative years both children yearned for nurturing from their parents, and not receiving it would have a lasting effect. As the oldest, Julie suffered far worse than her brother, who was too young to really appreciate what was going on.

The once happy-go-lucky little girl was fast becoming lost and insecure. She felt unloved and unable to depend on anyone. As Julie reached her ninth birthday, her world would collapse as her parents' marriage finally self-destructed.

In late 1976, John Scully began seeing an attractive female neighbor, who lived three doors away on North Palethorp Street. Over the last couple of years he had ceased to be interested in Julia, as she'd lost her looks and figure falling into a morass of drink and drugs. The one thing that had kept the marriage together for eleven years was their children, but now the tough policeman was looking for a way out.

"I'd come home from work and she'd be wasted," remembers John Scully. "Twice I had to call and have an emergency wagon take her to the hospital when she O.D.'d on her medicine. And I stayed with her for several years under that condition because of the children, but I knew I had to make another life."

On Julie's ninth birthday John Scully excused himself from her party, saying that he had to go to see a friend in New Jersey. But in the middle of the party Julia Scully happened to look out the window to see her husband kissing his new girlfriend in the street.

She flew out of the house in a fury to confront him. And to Julie's embarrassment her parents had a huge fight outside the house in front of her friends. There was a chilling silence at the party as John Scully rushed back in, packed a suitcase and stormed out of the house, never to return.

"I saw him with her across the street," said Julia. "That was the end of our marriage."

According to Julia, all their neighbors knew about her husband's affair. She was the last one to find out he was being unfaithful.

Today, John Scully claims he doesn't remember the exact circumstances of his leaving, but years later Julie would tell her future husband Tim Nist about it with tears in her eyes.

"I could measure her life by everything before that incident and afterwards," said Nist. "Everything she talked about fondly was before her ninth birthday and it was all bad times after that. It was like the extinction of one life and the start of some sort of great catastrophe."

CHAPTER THREE

GROWING UP IN FAMILY COURT

John Scully moved into a cheap apartment on North Front Street and resumed life as a bachelor. Although the children still saw him regularly, they were heartbroken that he had left. And they were traumatized as they found themselves right in the center of a bitter battle over their maintenance.

As Julia Scully had no job or income, she asked her estranged husband to support her and his children.

"He told me I could always go on welfare," said Julia. "It was very hard at that time as you had to get [the husband] to agree to pay child support. So I went on welfare to survive."

Throwing herself at the mercy of the Philadelphia Department of Public Welfare, Julia was granted $103.60 every two weeks to feed and clothe her children. According to Julia, John Scully never paid a cent towards their keep for eighteen months after he walked out.

Today, John Scully disputes that he was ever a dead-beat dad, and court papers reveal that he was paying $200 a month for his children's school tuition.

For the first few months after he left, the estranged couple argued constantly about John's access to his children. Reluctantly, Julia allowed him to take them camping in Dennisville Lake, where they had enjoyed so many good times in the past. But often without prior warning he would turn up at North Palethorp Street, spend an hour with the children and then leave.

In the wake of the break-up, Julia Scully began to fall apart as she desperately tried to cope with being a single mother. And as her drinking increased, so did the beatings.

"She was drinking too much," remembers John Junior, "and when something happened that pissed her off she would basically get something and beat Julie and me."

John says his mother also embarked on a campaign to poison his and Julie's minds against their father. "My mom would throw a road block so we couldn't see our father," remembers John Junior. "She would brainwash us into thinking that our dad didn't love us."

The sensitive Julie took her parents' separation far worse than her younger brother, although she remained stoic, never letting it show on the outside. After being constantly told by Julia that the father she adored didn't love her, she became terribly insecure. Her anxiety manifested itself in rebellion against her teachers at St. Boniface School.

As her school work began to deteriorate, her father stepped in. He enrolled her in the Holy Name Catholic school in Kensington, where he felt there would be tighter controls on his wayward daughter.

"Julie was a very intelligent girl," said her father. "She had no problems getting straight A's but then she started getting some bad marks at school so I sent her to a Catholic school."

For a while Julie calmed down and worked hard, getting good marks at the new school. But a few months later she began playing truant, spending her time with her friends hanging around at a local Dunkin' Donuts. Her photographic memory ensured that she still managed to remain at the top of the class, even though she rarely attended.

On September 8, 1978, Julia Scully, on the advice of her social worker, swore out a summons to the Philadelphia Common Pleas Court, demanding maintenance and child support from her husband. It would be the first salvo in an eight-year-long court battle between the Scullys, a battle that would see the children dragged through the Philadelphia Family Court system.

By this time John Scully had moved into a cheaper apartment on East Susquehanna Avenue, Philadelphia, with his new girlfriend, Lorelei, and her eight-year-old child. A court-appointed investigator checked out Scully's finances and a week later reported that the beat cop earned $335.44 a week before taxes.

At 10:00 a.m. on Thursday, October 5, John and Julia Scully and their children attended a Domestic Pleas hearing at the Philadelphia Family Court at 1801 Vine Street, in the center of the city. It was a bitter reunion for the Scullys but they finally managed to reach an agreement: John would pay $51 a week to support his family, to be automatically deducted from his wages every two weeks.

The following summer Julia, now thirty-five years old

and off welfare, decided to better herself. She enrolled in a day program at a local American Indian center to study for her General Education Diploma (GED), so she could get a job and have something to occupy her time. "I really wanted to get on with my life," said Julia. "I couldn't just sit home."

As Julia couldn't afford a baby-sitter there was no supervision for Julie, now eleven, and her nine-year-old brother, who were given complete freedom while their mother attended school. During their long summer vacation, John and Julie began to invite their friends over to the house to play. When Julia's watch, cash and other items began to disappear, she was furious and punished her children by grounding them.

"One time John and his cousin took fifteen dollars from my drawer and went off to play video games," said Julia. "We didn't have any money!"

Although John Junior agrees that he and Julie could be difficult when they were growing up, he claims that his mother often overreacted.

"We needed to be disciplined sometimes," he said. "But there were times, in my opinion, that she hit us for very minor things that could have been handled in another way."

One day Julia came home to discover that the children had raided her beer supply and were drinking. To teach them a lesson, she forced them to sit down in the kitchen and drink beer until they were sick.

The punishment did not work and Julie was already smoking and drinking with her friends. And it wouldn't be long before the girl would be totally out of control.

By the age of twelve Julie Scully had blossomed into a strikingly beautiful child. Taller than her classmates, the

dark-haired girl stood out from her friends with her perfect doe-eyed beauty. On the cusp of puberty, Julie began to realize that she was beautiful as she started to
attract the attention of the local boys.

Street-wise beyond her years, Julie began hanging out
on corners with friends listening to disco music and staying out to all hours.

"I'd tell her to come in at such-and-such a time and
she didn't," remembered Julia. "Then I'd be out there
looking for her and she didn't like that."

In 1980 Kensington was a tough neighborhood with
high unemployment and Julia was concerned that her
daughter would be exposed to drugs. One night a friend
of Julie's was staying over when Julia got up at midnight
to discover they had both disappeared. Alarmed, she
called the police to report Julie missing and then went
back to sleep. A few hours later the police picked up
Julie and her friend at a Dunkin' Donuts in downtown
Philadelphia and brought her home.

Julia was furious and once again grounded her daughter, forbidding her to go out at night.

"She was very unhappy about that," said Julia. "To
Julie it was always, if only her father was here things
would be different and everything would be all right."

Over the next few months Julie refused to obey her
mother, causing constant arguments about her going out.
Mother and daughter were equally stubborn and refused
to back down. They continually butted heads as each
refused to give in to the other.

In late 1980 Julia found a job repairing shoes at a
local factory. Now that she had a source of income,
things were easier, but she was finding it increasingly
difficult to control her children.

On one occasion Julie ran away for the weekend with

a friend. An anxious Julia searched the streets in vain for her daughter and was about to call the police when the friend's mother called to say that Julie was at her house.

When Julie finally came home, Julia was drunk and began to beat her. In tears, Julie fled the house and ran straight to her father, begging him to allow her to move in with him and his girlfriend Lorelei, whom he would later marry.

"She said her mom was always giving her a hard time," remembers John Scully. "So I said, 'Julie, you can come and live here but there are going to be certain rules.'"

The tough policeman, who had just moved into a new house on Almond Street in Philadelphia, then drew up a list of rules that Julie would have to obey if she wanted to live with him.

"I told her that I didn't want to see any fail marks on her report card," stated Scully, "and that I wanted her in the house by 9:30 p.m. [during weekday] nights. I said Friday and Saturday night, as long as I know where you're at—and I will verify it—you can be out until 11:00 p.m."

She also had to keep her bedroom tidy and help his girlfriend Lorelei with the dishes after meals. Before long the fiercely independent Julie, now thirteen, clashed with Lorelei. Julie was jealous of the other woman in her father's life, and whenever Lorelei laid down the law about doing the housework, an argument would ensue.

"Julie thought Lorelei was a drill instructor," said her father. "But she never hit her or anything."

As soon as Julie came to live with him, John Scully went to court and was granted legal custody of his daughter. Now that his sister had left, John Junior had to cope with his mother alone. The little boy became so miserable that after going on a camping trip to Dennisville Lake over Labor Day weekend with his father and sister, he begged them to let him stay, so he wouldn't have to return to his mother.

"He said, 'Dad, I've got to stay with you,' " said Scully. "I said, 'No problem, son.' Then I called my ex up and she was all for it."

A week after John moved in with his father, Julia Scully decided that she wanted her children back and went to court to argue her case. Listing her occupation as a student, Julia wrote on her petition: "I want the court to give me custody of my children."

On September 29, 1981, John and Julia Scully attended a preliminary hearing to determine the future of their children. In front of a judge, John accused Julia of beating the kids, saying they had come to him for protection and did not want to return to her.

"Both children now reside with their father," read the court report. "Father insisted on being granted custody, because the children have told him they want to live with him because their mother hollers at them and hits them too much."

An emotional Julia Scully strongly denied using any violence toward her children at the hearing. And when they failed to agree on custody, the matter was referred back to the Philadelphia Family Court.

"In my opinion the case will be protracted," wrote Julia's attorney Suzanne Fluhr, noting that John Scully, who was unrepresented, had made it clear he would fight for custody and call "at least four or five witnesses."

In December, Scully successfully petitioned the court to confirm his custody of the children and had it rubber-stamped. From now on Julia would only be able to see her children every other Saturday and Sunday between 12:00 p.m. and 4:00 p.m.

The judge also ruled that he John Scully no longer had to pay his estranged wife for the children's upkeep, although he was ordered to pay her $17 a week maintenance, suspended for thirty-two weeks as he had overpaid $544.

After John Scully's victory in court both children agreed they no longer wanted to see their mother. And over the next few weeks Julia desperately tried to see Julie and John, who refused to go and stay with her.

"When John was little he was mad at [his father]," reflected Julia many years later. "He blamed me and thought it was my fault. Although Julie said [our breakup] affected her, I never noticed it. But I never really gave it that much thought."

On January 3, 1982, Julie turned fourteen and her mother marked it by lodging a petition in family court for more access to her children. It was now five years since the Scullys had separated and they still had not filed for divorce.

In court papers Julia accused her estranged husband of not allowing her to see her children. She now asked the court for access to Julie and John on alternate weekends from 6:00 p.m. Friday until 7:00 p.m. Sunday. Claiming it was in the best interests of the children to spend more time with their mother, she requested "reasonable telephone access" and to have them for a month every summer and on alternate holidays.

In order to help the court reach a decision on their future, a psychiatrist was ordered to interview family members, and a social worker was sent to inspect Julia's home.

Julie was now becoming impossible for even her policeman father to control. Now in the eighth grade at Holy Name, she regularly played truant, preferring to go over to friends' houses to listen to pop music. And when John Scully found out he tried his best to rein her in.

"Julie wanted to do what *she* wanted to do," said Scully. "She was very headstrong and didn't want anybody to tell her anything."

Although Julie had always been close to her brother John, their almost two-year age difference now put distance between them, as they developed their own sets of friends. Over the next year they would drift further apart, even though they still saw each other every day at school.

"Going through high school, people definitely noticed how pretty Julie was," John Junior remembered. "She was a very charismatic person and she had a lot of friends."

But John Junior says that both children found their frequent appearances in family court an embarrassment and tried to keep them secret from friends. "It was a pain. I mean, I went to family court when I was with my mom, we went to family court when I was with my dad and he took over our custody. It was *real* embarrassing."

During a contempt of visitation hearing on May 2, 1982, Julie and John were asked by a judge which parent they would prefer to live with.

"Presently Julie is living with her father and likes it," read the report from the hearing. [She] claims mother would get drunk and beat children. Son, John is living with his father. [He] states mother drank and hit them."

Also present at the hearing was Julia Scully who became highly emotional on hearing her children say they didn't want to live with her. At one point she broke down in tears and pledged to fight and win them back, whatever the consequences.

It would be another month before Julia Scully next saw her children in the offices of Philadelphia psychiatrist Dr. Fredric D. Shecter. One by one Julia and her children went in to see Dr. Shecter for a psychiatric evaluation so the court could decide where to place John and Julie. It was a humiliating day for all of them as they laid bare the sorry state of the Scully family.

First to be interviewed was Julie, whom Dr. Shecter described as "attractive" and "thin" with a cascade of shoulder-length brown hair. She was casually dressed and wearing black-rimmed glasses. Softly spoken, Julie appeared "cooperative and amiable," telling the psychiatrist from the outset that she would not visit her mother.

"Joy was expressed in terms of living with dad," Dr. Shecter later noted in his report for the family court. "and resentment towards mother for her drinking and fighting with Julie and her brother."

He found the pretty teenager to be highly intelligent and "goal-oriented" with no hint of psychosis. The only problems he could detect were "typical age adequate conflicts of adolescence" and issues arising out of her dysfunctional family relationships.

Julie also told Dr. Shecter about the abuse she suffered at home and her feelings of abandonment. "Mom used to beat us," Julie sadly told the psychiatrist. "Dad and Mom separated because Dad was cheating with another woman."

When asked about Holy Name School, where she was now in the eighth grade, Julie seemed ambivalent.

"I like the school but not the teachers," she said. "I

like to learn and want to be a computer programmer."

She told Dr. Shecter that she and her friends like to go to movies and dances and did not take drugs or drink alcohol, "but we're not goody-goodies," she pointed out.

When questioned about living with her father, Julie replied, "we rarely fight," adding that she was reprimanded if she didn't do her chores.

In his report, Dr. Shecter noted Julie's fear, anger and resentment towards her mother, advising against lengthy visitations. He also warned that if Julie was forced to see her mother against her will "she may well respond with increased negativism and resistance, which would lead to greater difficulty."

When her twelve-year-old brother entered the office, Dr. Shecter observed that he appeared anxious, keeping his hands in his pockets throughout the interview. Although the brown-haired young boy flashed an engaging smile, Dr. Shecter felt that he was being cautious.

"Neither [of us] likes to be with Mom," John told the doctor. "She drinks and then keeps us up all night and makes us do chores. [She's] always asking us questions and punishing us. She's always hollering and trying to upset us."

The bright, good-natured boy told the doctor that although he was "uncertain" about his future, he wanted to finish school and find a job involving nuclear power.

Then he was asked to give three wishes. John replied that firstly, he would like a million dollars; secondly, a yacht for Dad; and thirdly, for him, Julie and their father to all go to Florida on a vacation.

He stated he had no wish to see his mother, and that she didn't play any part in his future hopes and dreams.

After the interview John came out and sat next to his big sister. Then their mother, who was waiting outside anxiously, was summoned into the doctor's office. Although Julia attempted to put on a brave face for the occasion, the hardship and suffering she was going through was obvious.

"Mrs. Scully is a thirty-nine-year-old American Indian woman with short black hair, dark eyes, slightly obese, but a pleasant appearance," Dr. Shecter later reported. As Julia began to discuss her failed marriage and her relationship to her children, Dr. Shecter noted that she was overtaken by "a saddened or isolated mood" verging on melancholy.

"Issues centered on the marital separation from John Scully six-years-ago [sic] when he was cheating. Since then, the children lived with her, but mom had difficulty setting limits, particularly with Julie, and last year it got to a point where she had to ask Mr. Scully to take Julie. Eventually he took John Junior.

"Mom relates that she was attending the Cedar Program to become a shoe repairer and could not give the children the necessary guidance."

Although Julia said she did not "quarrel" with her husband having custody, she still wanted to visit her children so they could have a relationship.

"She knows Julie does not want to see her, but feels John Jr. might," wrote the doctor.

In his diagnosis of Julia, Dr. Shecter could not detect any mental disorder but put her problems down to "phase of life circumstances."

In his recommendations to family court, Dr. Shecter wrote: "Mrs. Scully is dealing with a difficult situation. She is aware that her children do not wish to visit with her and can accept this intellectually, but emotionally it presents conflict."

He suggested that visits be gradually introduced, but

not forced on the children. And he also advised that Julia receive "counseling" from the social service agency to help her properly interact with her children so they could develop "trust and security in mom."

However, his report ended on a cautionary note: "If alcohol intake is an issue, hopefully, this will be worked on."

Two weeks later John Scully angrily hit back by filing a court petition demanding that Julia now pay him $70 a week maintenance for the children as she was now working.

CHAPTER FOUR

LOST CHILDHOOD

Ironically, it would be Julie Scully who would ultimately want to move back with her mother and repair their relationship. She disliked her father's girlfriend intensely, resisting any attempts to regulate her behavior. And as Julie became more and more unhappy, she rebelled by running away to friends for days at a time. At one point her behavior became so bad that there was a motion for the court to declare her "incorrigible."

Although she was still fourteen, Julie was sophisticated way beyond her years. Tall and thin, she now had the perfect, well-endowed body of a mature woman and turned heads wherever she went. She had long given up ever finding the love and attention she so craved from her family, seeking it instead from the friends who became her emotional support network.

After Julie graduated from Holy Name in the summer of 1982, her father was concerned for her future education, taking steps to ensure she would get the best.

One morning he put on his police uniform and went to see the principal of the local high school that he had carefully selected for Julie.

But while he was waiting he struck up a conversation with another parent, who began telling him about the new High School of Engineering and Science, then affiliated with Philadelphia's prestigious Temple University. The school was for exceptionally gifted pupils and there and then John Scully decided it was where his daughter belonged.

But there were hurdles to face, as the High School of Engineering and Science only took academically gifted pupils. So Scully ruthlessly lobbied to get Julie accepted, pushing the fact that his daughter should be classed as a "minority," being half American Indian.

"I figured a lot of other people were using that," he reasoned, "so I might as well for my daughter."

Opened three years earlier in the old Temple University Technology building on the corner of Broad Street and Columbia, just two hundred new pupils were admitted annually into the ninth grade. As part of its mission statement the school aimed to recruit high-achieving students from around Philadelphia to "learn and grow" in an atmosphere of mutual respect for "all ethnic groups and multi-cultures."

Academic standards were high and a school prospectus boasted that "ninety-five percent of the students leave to grace the finest institutions in the country," listing Yale, Princeton and Harvard as examples. With her stated desire for a career in computers, John Scully could not have found a better high school for his daughter.

So in September 1983, Julie passed the required mathematics and English placement tests and was accepted as a pupil, to the delight of her father, who dreamed of her getting a college education and going into the professions. But although Julie was highly ambitious and goal-oriented, she had a short attention span and found it hard to concentrate on one thing at a time.

Also starting at the school that day was fourteen-year-old Mary Jones (not her real name), who would soon become close friends with Julie, as they attended classes together. On the surface the two girls had little in common. Mary was a serious, highly ambitious student, who would go on to become a dental surgeon, while Julie always put partying first and her lessons a distant second.

"She was a little wild," remembers Mary. "She skipped school a lot and she used to hang out with a partying crowd."

During her first semester Julie made many new friends and began playing truant, spending school days at their homes. Before long John Scully received a telephone call from the school, complaining about Julie's bad attendance record and asking him to do something about it.

"That's when I started having problems with her," he said. "I would take her down to school and she would walk in through the front door and out the back. I thought she was at school and she wouldn't go."

Most days she would go to friends' houses to talk and play music, but she also loved slipping off alone to the Philadelphia Museum of Art, where she would spend hours looking at the pictures and exhibits. "I always liked to go there when I was little," she would reminisce years later. "It's so quiet and it smells old."

Julie's truancy caused a major rift with her father, who saw her deliberately destroying her one opportunity for a good education. On several occasions, after heated arguments, she ran away from home for days at a time.

But even if she was not attending many classes, her work hardly suffered: Julie's photographic memory allowed her to read school books the night before a test and then ace the examination.

"She was so brilliant," said Mary Jones. "She would disappear from school for about a month and show up on the day of the chemistry exam and get a ninety-eight. And I studied and I would get a C."

As Mary got to know Julie better, she spoke about the break-up of her parents' marriage, complaining that her father's girlfriend had rejected her and she no longer felt comfortable in their house. Mary began to realize that her friend was deeply unhappy and constantly looking for the next quick fix, the next night of excitement.

"That's why Julie ran away a bunch of times during school," said Mary. "She used to hang out with a little partying crowd and she was always on the go and had to be the center of attention."

Julie had recently discovered sex and Mary saw her go through a series of short-lived, often obsessive, relationships with older boys. It would always start off with her thinking she had found true love but she quickly became bored, moving on to a new boyfriend.

"Julie always had a man in her life," explained Mary. "There was one serious boyfriend but then it was one after another."

In July 1983, Julie, now fifteen, ran away from her father's home for the final time, never to return. During the weeks she was missing, John Scully made no attempt to find her, never even filing a missing persons report.

When she finally telephoned her father, saying that she now wanted to live with her mother, he readily agreed. After all the tension between his girlfriend and Julie, he was somewhat relieved to see her go. However,

John Junior would remain with his father until joining the U.S. Navy some years later.

John Scully Senior had taken Julie at her word that she would move back with Julia, but several months later he discovered she had actually been living with a school friend named Angie in south Philadelphia. Just two days before Julie was due to return for her second year at the High School of Engineering and Science, Angie's mother telephoned Julia to tell her that Julie was living with them. Then Julie came on the line to announce that she wanted to move back.

"I told her to come home," said Julia. "And she came back to live with me."

By the time Julie moved back in with her mother, the dynamic in their always-difficult relationship had drastically changed. Instead of Julia looking after her daughter, it was now the other way around. And from that point there developed a curious co-dependence between them.

"She took care of the person who had abused her," explains John Junior, who observed from a distance. "In my opinion it was a side-effect of what happened to her in childhood."

With her mother out to work all day and often medicated at night, Julie had absolute freedom and could do whatever she wanted. Now she hardly bothered to go to school at all, staying out all night while Julia desperately telephoned her friends all over north Philadelphia trying to track her down.

"Finally, I got really angry at her," remembers Julia. "I said, 'Julie, all you want to do is party. That's the only reason you go to school.' But there was nothing I could do."

Julia was also concerned that her wayward daughter

might be doing drugs, but when she tackled her on the subject Julie strongly denied it, saying she merely drank alcohol and smoked cigarettes.

In late 1983, Julia was officially granted custody of Julie. In an eight-point petition to court she had accused John Scully of failing to provide proper supervision for Julie or make any attempt to find her after she had disappeared. She demanded that he pay $85 a week for Julie's room and board; a court would trim it to $63.

Scully replied by officially filing for divorce, so he could marry his long-time girlfriend Lorelei and get Julia out of his life once and for all.

On April 4, 1984, John Scully was officially granted a divorce on the grounds that Julia had violated her marriage vows by offering such indignities to John as to "make his condition intolerable and life burdensome."

After almost nineteen years of marriage—seven of which had been spent apart after Julia caught him with another woman—the final divorce papers would officially list John Scully as the wronged party.

He now lost touch with the daughter who had once so adored him. And they would not see each other for another four years.

That September, Julie dropped out of the School of Engineering and Science to make her own way in the world. She found herself an office job and her father immediately applied to family court for permission to stop paying any further maintenance toward her keep.

Now that she was earning a wage, Julie finally had the freedom to indulge her passion for new clothes, make-up and jewelry. She loved going out shopping with her girlfriends and trying on the latest fashions. Shop employees would often remark that she should become a model, with her stunning, five-foot, seven-inch body, perfect sculptured face and radiant smile.

Julie was now hardly ever at her mother's North Palethorp Street house, spending most of her time with her friends who were scattered around Philadelphia and New Jersey. The only time she came home was to have her mother do her laundry.

"She kind of bounced around from one group of friends to another," remembered Mary Jones, who had remained close to Julie after they had both left the School of Engineering and Science. "I didn't hang out with them too much because I didn't have a car at the time, so there was a separation there."

In early 1985, Julie fell in love with a young electrician named Neal Ziegler, whom she'd met through mutual friends. She was instantly attracted to the tall, handsome man, six-years her senior. They soon embarked on a passionate love affair.

Neal came from a good family who lived in Moorestown, one of the most exclusive towns in southern New Jersey. Julia Scully thoroughly approved of the match when her daughter announced that they planned to get married.

"Neal is a very gentle person," said Mary Jones. "He cared about Julie a lot."

In November 1985, two months before her eighteenth birthday, Julie and Neal were married in a small church ceremony. It would be almost a year before the bride's father was even told that his seventeen-year-old daughter had gotten married.

To Julie, Neal meant emotional and financial security and a chance to break free from her needy mother, who was always on her case. Years later, Julie would look

back and regret that she had jumped into marriage so
early and missed out on her youth.

The newlyweds settled down in an apartment across
the Ben Franklin Bridge in New Jersey, as Julie adapted
to her new role as wife. The couple were very much in
love but storm clouds soon gathered on their romantic
horizon.

On January 3, 1986, Julie turned eighteen and the Philadelphia Family Court declared that she had reached the
age of majority, scrapping all outstanding petitions for
maintenance from her parents. After nine years of almost
continual family court proceedings, Julie Scully was finally free of her parents' ongoing legal battles.

In the early days of their marriage, Julie and Neal
often visited Julia Scully in Kensington, if they happened to be in Philadelphia seeing friends.

"By then at least I knew where she was," said Julia.

That summer, Julie brought her new husband to Philadelphia to meet her father, who had no idea his daughter had even married. On meeting Neal, John Scully was
delighted, believing that he was the sort of man who
would "straighten out" his daughter.

"I thought he was a real nice guy," said Scully. "He
was mild-mannered and I liked him."

Scully was much impressed with the fact that Neal's
father was a retired doctor, who now taught medical
studies at a college. He felt he would be a good influence
on Julie and gave the couple his blessing.

But a year after they married Julie walked out on
Neal, moving back in with her mother. Julie's loud, extroverted personality, and her constant need to be the
center of attention totally overpowered the quieter and
more reserved Neal. She was also becoming bored with

his dope-smoking friends, saying that she couldn't relate to them.

Julia Scully says her daughter told her that one particular argument with Neal had turned violent and she walked out on him.

"They were young," said Julia. "Julie told me she had tried smoking dope but didn't care for it."

In spring 1988, Julie decided to give the marriage a second chance and went back to Neal. But six months later she walked out forever, filing for an annulment.

"She became bored," said Mary Jones, who was close to the couple, "and didn't want to be married anymore."

Julie moved back in with her mother but once again there were constant arguments as she resumed her old life of partying and staying out all night and using her mother's house as a hotel.

Julie was now working in an insurance office, investigating accident claims and making good money. But Julia says she spent most of it on clothes, never once offering to contribute anything toward her keep.

Always passionate about sports, Julie regularly attended games at a local hockey league, where she was the official scorekeeper. At one winter game a girlfriend of hers was keeping score when she was sworn at by a player. Julie immediately sprang to her defense, challenging him over the insult.

When the six-footer refused to back down, Julie began hitting him. The referee stopped the game as everyone turned to watch the spectacle taking place in the hockey ring. Later Julie would often triumphantly relive the fight, telling friends her only regret was that the thick mittens she was wearing had softened the blows.

That winter Julie moved down the shore to Avalon, New Jersey, to share an apartment with a girlfriend. She began dating a young man from Kentucky, and enthusiastically threw herself into the short-lived new relationship.

Julie's beauty was now undeniable. Wherever she went people stared and she was well aware of the power she had over men. She loved flirting with her many admirers and seemed to bathe in the attention they gave her.

The vulnerable little girl inside was desperately searching for the love and security she had never known. It wouldn't be long before a new man came into her life, and would change it forever.

CHAPTER FIVE

STABILITY

If Julie Scully's childhood was troubled and insecure, Tim Nist's was exactly the opposite. The youngest child of William and Margaret Nist, Tim grew up with his three elder sisters just outside Princeton, New Jersey, in a stable, middle-class family environment, sailing through his boyhood without a care in the world.

"It was as good as families can be," says Tim. "I mean, we stuck together."

Born in Ohio, Bill Nist had moved to New Jersey as a young man and founded a successful agricultural company, manufacturing and selling fertilizer and pesticides. His New York–born wife Margaret was a homemaker, who instilled a sense of discipline into her children that would help them succeed in the world.

The Nist children all attended high school in the university town of Princeton, and after graduating Tim studied civil engineering in Trenton, before dropping out to start earning a living.

Even as a student Tim had an eye for business, buying, repairing, and then reselling automobiles to make extra money. In his early twenties the athletically handsome six-foot, four-inch Nist had worked a variety of jobs as a cook, bartender, waiter and at one time as a disc jockey in a night club near Trenton.

In his late twenties, Tim decided to concentrate on starting his own business and making money. It was the late 1980s with the real estate boom in full swing in New Jersey. Using what he had learned from his father's fertilizer plant, he started his own landscaping business, called Stirling Lawns. Tim was in the right place at the right time and his lawn manicuring service was soon in great demand.

"I was probably the best at what I did," he says. "A lot of new homes were being built for two-income families. and they didn't have a lot of spare time so they hired me to take care of their lawns."

Working out of his condo in Hamilton, New Jersey, Tim hired a small staff, including a secretary and several lawn specialists and soon had clients all over the Mercer and Monmouth County areas.

His easy charm and humor always ensured that he had plenty of girlfriends. By the time he turned thirty, Tim had been engaged several times, but had so far resisted walking down the aisle. Then, on Saturday, July 8, 1989, he was at a party at the swank Bordentown Yacht Club, drinking with friends when he saw Julie Scully and was immediately struck by her unusual, exotic looks.

At first he watched Julie from a distance and asked his friends if they knew her. Finally he seized his chance when Julie, who was casually dressed in a tee-shirt and baggy jeans, pulled out a cigarette and put it in her mouth.

"I swung into action and gave her a light," said Tim. "And so we got talking and spent the rest of the evening bombing around in my black Porsche 928, visiting friends."

The next day he invited her to go surfing with him at the Jersey shore the following weekend. Julie accepted, immediately calling up several friends to tell them about the handsome man who had asked her out on a date. She would later use the date she first met Tim as the PIN number for all her credit cards, saying it brought her good luck.

The next weekend Tim collected twenty-one-year-old Julie from her apartment, and they drove to the shore. It was a beautiful hot summer day and Tim asked Julie about herself during the journey. Although he was eleven years older, the couple had an instant rapport, finding they shared the same quirky sense of humor.

Later on the beach Julie took off her sweat shirt to reveal a sexy bikini adorning her perfect body.

"I said, 'Wow! where was this hiding?'" reminisced Tim of the first time he saw Julie in a swimsuit. "She was a total babe really and I thought she was Asian. Later I found out she was Navajo."

Over the next few months Tim and Julie were inseparable, spending all their spare time together. They shared a passion for ice hockey and would go to New Jersey Devils games and then go drinking in the bars around Trenton.

Other nights they would go to Tim's condominium where Julie would prepare supper. Then they'd sit on the couch watching romantic old movies like *Casa-*

blanca and *Gone With the Wind*, which Julie had never seen before.

To Tim the eleven-year age difference was never a problem. He felt more experienced and worldly than Julie, and became her mentor, introducing her to a fast new life of adventure and travel. He enjoyed being able to relive his favorite things and experience them again through Julie's innocent eyes.

Julie, who had never felt that she could rely on her real father, began to see Tim Nist as a secure father-figure who could protect her. Initially, Tim wasn't interested in being in any long-term relationship, but Julie's persuasive beauty soon made him reconsider.

That St. Patrick's Day, Tim Nist discovered just how tough and competitive Julie could be about getting her own way.

"Julie could be a real roughhouse," remembers Tim. "I was sitting in a bar, innocently talking to a blonde girl when she came in. I didn't even see her and the next thing I know Julie punched me hard in the face and gave me a black eye."

When he recovered his composure enough to ask Julie why she had hit him, she replied, "First I'll kick her ass for talking to you and then I'll kick her ass for being a blonde."

Throughout their relationship there would be a double-standard where it was OK for Julie to talk to guys, but on no account could Tim ever talk to a girl without incurring Julie's wrath.

"Julie was brought up on the streets of Philadelphia and she did have a temper," explained Tim. "She was much younger than me and there were emotional situations."

Tim viewed Julie as the quintessential alpha female

with himself as an alpha male. He told her they were born to lead the pack, and the world would be their oyster if they only put their minds to it and didn't screw up.

A few weeks later Julie was sitting at her desk at the law firm where she worked in Lawrenceville, New Jersey, when a secretary showed her an advertisement in *The Trentonian* newspaper, recruiting local girls for its upcoming beauty contest. The secretary remarked that Julie should enter, so she cut out the ad and put it in her bag.

That evening, despite some reservations, Julie showed it to Tim, who became very enthusiastic. Having once worked as a photographer, he immediately offered to take the picture and sent Julie upstairs to change into a swimsuit.

"It was a lark," he says. "She asked which bathing suit she should wear so I told her to wear the one she had worn surfing on our first date."

The following day Tim sent in the photograph to *The Trentonian*, but it would be weeks before they got a response.

Tim ran his landscaping business out of a small office in his Hamilton condominium. One day he arrived back to find that his secretary was gone and Julie was sitting at her desk with an enigmatic smile. When Tim asked where his secretary was, Julie just said, "She left."

Tim suspected that Julie had resorted to sabotage by saying something offensive to make his secretary quit. Later when he asked her, she denied it.

"Sometimes women can speak their own language," he explained. "Julie was kind of like, 'Beat it.'"

From that day, Julie started working as office manager for Stirling Lawns and over the next few months she introduced computers to efficiently reorganize his growing business.

"I used to do hand ledgers," said Tim. "Julie came up with all the systems in the office. I left that to her completely. I'm the type of boss that likes to delegate."

Julie moved into Tim's Hamilton condo in the spring of 1990. To their friends they seemed a perfect couple, managing to combine working together with a romantic relationship.

Julie loved Tim's confidence and stability, telling friends he was going places. For the first time since her parents had split up, she was happy.

"Tim gave her independence," said her old school friend, Mary Jones. "Because she married so young the first time, there were a lot of things she missed out on, like being a single young adult woman. He acknowledged that and agreed to let her have the freedom that she wanted."

But although Mary and her other friends weren't concerned with the age difference, Julia Scully had reservations about her daughter dating a man eleven years older.

"I knew that if I didn't approve there would be an argument," said her mother. "By then I had figured out that if Julie wanted to do something, she did it."

When Julia got laid off from her shoe repair job in May, Julie asked her to come to Hamilton and help her distribute the new fliers she'd designed for Stirling Lawns. Each day they would take Tim's Porsche and tour the new housing developments, placing the fliers in the front doors.

"She seemed very happy with Tim at that time," said

Julia. "But she worked hard for him and was always in the office. I often thought Tim didn't recognize what she did."

Though Julie and her mother had mended their bridges and were finally getting closer, the old family acrimony resurfaced when John Junior brought his new wife Laura and their son to Tim's house to meet his family. Two years earlier, John had joined the Navy and had been stationed in Florida before moving to a base in upstate New York.

Since their school days, John and Julie had only seen each other sporadically, but he hadn't seen his mother for many years. That summer, flushed with her own happiness with Tim, Julie decided to try and reunite her mother and brother, inviting them to visit.

At first everything went well as they caught up with their lives and agreed to keep in closer touch in the future. But two months later Julia suddenly telephoned her son and began asking him difficult questions about his early childhood, before he had moved in with his father.

"She was drunk," remembered John. "We got into an argument after she said some things about my wife."

John was furious, and after putting the phone down, called Julie to complain about their mother's behavior. When Julie sided with her mother, a heated argument ensued. It would be another four years before Julie spoke to her brother again.

By June, Julie had still not heard from *The Trentonian* about her picture and was becoming impatient. Finally, she couldn't contain herself any longer and marched down to the newspaper's offices on Perry Street in Trenton, demanding to speak to the editor.

"That was Julie," said Tim. "She went in and said,

'Yo ... what gives! Why isn't my picture in the paper?' "

The astonished editor sat her down at his desk and told her to calm down, explaining that she had already been selected as a finalist in the competition and her picture would soon be appearing on Page 6. Overjoyed, Julie drove straight home to tell Tim the good news and to start preparing for the competition.

CHAPTER SIX

MODEL

The Second Annual *Trentonian* Swimwear Contest was a modest affair. Several hundred guests filed into the Marriott Hotel courtyard in Market Fair, Princeton, on a hot Saturday afternoon to see a dozen female finalists compete for a trip to California and a chance to enter the Ujena Bikini Jam.

Julie Scully had thought of little else since her picture had finally appeared on *The Trentonian's* Page 6 several weeks earlier. Her busty 36B swimsuit pose had attracted a lot of attention in Hamilton and the prospect of being a model had given her a new purpose in life.

Since then she had spent most of her spare time selecting the sexy swimsuit she would wear for the competition, and practicing her posing in front of a full-length mirror. Tim had been very encouraging, giving her advice on how to improve her runway walk and answer the personality phase of the competition.

"I remember us joking around when she asked me to

suggest three words to give the judges to describe her," said Tim. "I said, 'skinny, big tits.' "

By the time they arrived at the mall, Julie was brimming with confidence, ready for her moment in the spotlight. As she joined the other girls in the Marriott Hotel changing room, Tim dutifully took his place near the stage, which had been decked out as a runway with colorful cardboard palm trees and beach umbrellas.

At 3:00 p.m. the emcee, from a local radio station that was co-hosting the event with *The Trentonian*, strode on stage. After some brief announcements he started to introduce the girls, as the crowd rose to its feet to applaud.

Waiting nervously in the wings was Julie Scully, who would be one of the last girls to go down the runway. One by one the finalists took the stage to parade their perfect, tanned bodies to a cacophony of cheers and catcalls from their supporters in the audience.

One of the judges was last year's winner, Cheryl Chuplis, who would soon become a good friend of Julie's.

"I thought Julie was the most beautiful girl there," says Chuplis, who is now a professional model and actress. "She was just so striking. At first I thought she was Asian and I was trying to figure out what nationality she was."

Although Cheryl marked Julie down as a winner her fellow judges did not agree and she went unplaced, having to console herself with some vouchers from a local store.

"Julie was pissed," remembered Tim. "She came down to our table, saying she was far better than the girl who had won."

But even though she had not won this time, Julie had certainly made an impression on *Trentonian* editor Gale

Baldwin, who told his staff to hire her for their Page 6 promotions team.

The modeling competition would mark the start of a three-year roller-coaster ride for Julie, changing her life forever. The once-insecure girl adored all the attention lavished upon her for her stunning body, and lapped up the approval. She loved being in the spotlight and resolved to use her exposure in *The Trentonian* as a stepping stone to a future modeling career.

And she didn't have long to wait. Later that summer the Trenton-based Hub City beer distributors called *The Trentonian*, asking them to suggest a couple of Page 6 models who could add some glamour to their local bar and club promotions.

"They approached me about working for them," said Cheryl Chuplis. "And they also approached Julie. I'm a blonde and I guess they needed a brunette."

Soon Cheryl and Julie were working three or four nights a week as good-will ambassadors for Miller Brewing Company and Coors Light, touring all over the South Jersey Shore. Julie's vibrant personality and outgoing nature made her a natural for the job. Night after night she would network, charming the local beer distributors and bar owners.

Julie and Cheryl would often stay long after the official promotion finished, happily chatting with Hub City clients late into the night. Although Julie often flirted through her natural sense of humor, she always went home to Tim.

"Julie would light up a room," said Chuplis. "We would talk to every single person about promoting a product, and be the last ones to leave."

During those first early promotion nights a close friendship developed between the two models. They became a team, developing a following among the local baseball players who would come to see them.

"We'd give them our schedule," Cheryl laughed. "And we'd hang out with them afterwards. It was so much fun."

Most days Julie would call up Cheryl for girl-talk. They would deliberate about what they would wear for that evening's event and discuss how the previous ones had gone. They talked about their dreams and ambitions and for the first time in her life Julie seemed to have some real direction.

She still worked full-time in Tim's office and business was booming. The summer period was the busiest and after Julie would finish her Stirling Lawns work she would jump in her car to drive to that evening's modeling assignment.

"Julie networked her way into doing all kinds of promotional stuff," said Tim, who was proud of her success. "She went on shoots for *The Trentonian* and did some posters, calendars and charity work for the Sunshine Foundation."

Tim rarely attended the promotional nights, preferring to stay at home with his pet dog D.J., or to pursue his hobbies: competing in model rocket tournaments, and taking part in Civil War re-enactments.

One day Julie asked her mother to take the train down to Hamilton as she had something to show her. After picking Julia up at the station, Julie was driving home when she suddenly pointed up at a large billboard towering over the highway.

"It was Julie in a swimsuit advertising *The Trentonian*," says Julia Scully. "She wanted to surprise me. She was so happy and proud to show me."

The billboard stayed up for two months and Julie

loved driving past it and pointing it out to friends. It also boosted her career, leading to a string of new modeling assignments after local auto dealers and other companies called the paper to hire her.

The photographer who had taken the shot for the billboard was *Trentonian* staff photographer Tom Kelly and Julie soon became his favorite model. Kelly, who had won a Pulitzer Prize for his 1979 photo coverage of a hostage situation in East Coventry Township, Pennsylvania, now specialized in taking most of the paper's Page 6 sexy swimsuit shots.

"Julie liked the camera and the camera liked her," says Kelly. "She had that something that set her apart from the other girls. She was a total professional and never allowed herself to be photographed or viewed in any way that wasn't wholesome. I mean, there were some photographs that appeared in *The Trentonian* over the years that I don't think were quite wholesome. One thing about Julie, she wouldn't allow any kind of pose that didn't portray her in a very nice light."

Over the next few months Kelly got to know Julie and Tim well through the paper's various charity softball games and the other promotional events they worked on together. Although some of the other Page 6 girls could be notoriously difficult on shoots, Julie always went the extra mile to help. That endeared her to Kelly and his editors.

"She was my favorite," says Kelly. "There were a couple of girls that they liked because they worked well with us. And Julie was right at the top of the list."

In the two years since *Trentonian* publisher Sandy Schwartz introduced near-naked swimsuit models to his Page 6, circulation had risen ten percent, to about eighty-thousand copies a day. Unlike its rivals, *The Trentonian* did not have a subscriber base, depending solely on newsstand sales.

"The whole thing started as an effort to build a stable of models that we could use for special sections, rather than getting transparencies from agencies," explained Schwartz, who has now left the paper and moved to Florida. "We used Julie a hell of a lot because she was accessible. A lot of these girls were pretty flaky and unreliable and some of them developed pretty inflated [egos] and forgot who made them famous. Julie wasn't like that at all."

As *The Trentonian*'s Page 6 became something of a local institution, Julie Scully quickly became a celebrity around Trenton. She loved being recognized in the street and restaurants and began getting invited to many civic events and fund-raisers, where she became friends with the Mayor and other civic leaders.

She was also a star player on the *Trentonian* softball team. While the other Page 6 girls tended to sit on the sidelines trying to look beautiful, Julie literally threw herself into the games.

"Julie was out there in a pair of shorts and a halter-top chasing down fly balls," remembers *Trentonian* city editor Paul Micole. "I remember watching her and thinking, 'She's got no fear.' It said so much about her."

By the fall of 1990, the seasonal promotion work for the beer companies was slowing down so Julie started entering local beauty contests, winning a string of titles. Competing on the tough New York/Philadelphia beauty circuit, Julie was soon making an average of $500 a week as a beauty queen, with a host of titles including Miss Muscle Cars, Miss Hawaiian Tropic, New Jersey and Miss Beach Haven.

"First Julie and I had to learn about the industry,"

explained Tim Nist. "There is, of course, high fashion and there's bikini modeling and the girls' bodies are completely different."

At five-foot, seven-inches Julie was too short for fashion work, so she concentrated on the bikini end, pretending that she was two inches shorter to fit the height requirements. But she and Tim soon found that the career path for a pin-up beauty queen was limited if, like Julie, she refused to take her clothes off, as some of the other Page 6 girls had.

"You can do television ads with the cheesecake pictures," Tim said. "If you want to go into the extremes there is nude photography, but Julie wanted nothing to do with that."

With her successful new career Julie was happier than she had ever been. Now finally getting the attention and approval she had craved for so long, she possessed a new confidence and positive outlook on her life.

As her marriage to Neal Ziegler had recently been annulled, Julie decided that she wanted to marry Tim, embarking on a campaign to force a marriage proposal by Christmas.

"It had always been discussed," said Tim. "But Julie wanted an engagement ring. She was pretty persistent and she finally won me. I was moving along with my life in a smooth sea and she was headstrong and that's what she wanted. She was a very controlling person."

In the weeks leading up to Christmas 1990, Julie began to fear that Tim might not propose. She discussed it at length with her new friend Cheryl Chuplis, during their promotional nights.

"This was really important to her," remembers Chuplis. "She kept talking about him getting her an engagement ring and getting married. In fact, she was starting to get a little aggravated at one point, wondering if they were going to get engaged."

Then, early on Christmas morning, a triumphant Julie telephoned Cheryl to wake her up with the news that Tim had just proposed and given her a ring.

"She was so excited," remembered Cheryl. "She was like a giggling schoolgirl."

Straight after Christmas Julie began planning the wedding, determined that it would be a gala event where she would shine as never before. That spring she was a whirl of activity, checking out local halls for the reception and organizing the menu down to the last nut.

Her father was now back in her life and had agreed to contribute a thousand dollars to the wedding, after a somewhat uneasy first meeting with his new prospective son-in-law. Tim Nist and John Scully came from different worlds and his daughter was aching to make the transition from her blue-collar Philadelphia roots to a life of wealth and ease.

Five years earlier John Scully had married his longtime girlfriend Lorelei and retired from the Philadelphia Police Department. He moved to Delaware where his pension went further, finding a job as a security supervisor at Delaware Technical College.

Soon after Julie had moved in with Tim they drove down to Delaware to see her father. It was a tense meeting as the two men had little in common.

"Tim would always give me an abrupt answer," said John Scully. "He was sociable enough but he couldn't just bullshit with you. I'd do what I could. I'd always offer him drinks and that, but there was no small talk. I liked her first husband a lot better."

Tim got on far better with Julie's mother and the two

of them struck up a good relationship. But when Julia Scully heard that her daughter planned to marry a man eleven years older, she warned Julie that he would be set in his ways and that she shouldn't expect him to change.

Julia also gave Tim some words of advice in her own inimitable fashion, saying: "If you marry someone young like her, you better put on your dancing shoes."

That April, Julie threw herself into modeling with a vengeance, determined to earn the extra thousands of dollars required for her November wedding. Tim was given little say in the planning, merely submitting a list of his family and friends, which Julie promptly edited.

"Again it was the whole control thing," said Tim. "She wanted to make sure it was to her liking and she had her own definite ideas."

In her second year as a professional model Julie Scully seemed to be everywhere, working five or six nights a week as well as her day job for Tim. On April 16, Julie appeared on Page 6 of *The Trentonian* in a white polka dot bikini. Listing her occupation as an "office manager," Julie said that her goal in life was to become a successful actress and her hobby was hunting for fossils.

On Wednesday, June 12, Julie competed in her second *Trentonian* Swimwear Contest. This year it was a far grander evening affair at the Hyatt-Regency Princeton Ballroom.

Julie and Tim had invited their friends to cheer her on from the table they had reserved by the stage. But for the second year running Julie was disappointed at not winning, having to make do with a free swimsuit and a year's tennis membership to the Hillsborough Country Club.

Two weeks later her picture was prominently featured throughout *The Trentonian*'s annual "Down the Shore" supplement, posing at the various beach resorts around the Jersey Shore. By now Julie was gathering quite a following of local fans and was much involved in her charity work for the Jersey branch of the Sunshine Foundation, which raises money to send terminally ill children to Disney World and on other dream vacations.

With her modeling career taking off, Julie now focused on New York to try and make it as an actress. After sending out a batch of black-and-white headshots, she landed a minor role appearing in HBO documentary trailers.

"She wanted to push it a little more," says Cheryl Chuplis. "What was holding her back was that she was so busy working the office for Tim, especially the spring and summer which was the height of their season. And boy, she was non-stop."

At this point Julie was torn between becoming a full-time model and possibly an actress, and her day job. Always insecure, Julie worried that if she left Stirling Lawns, Tim would get another female secretary who could become a rival for his affection.

"Modeling full-time would take her away from me and I don't think she wanted to relinquish that hold," explained Tim. "She just didn't want anyone else in there working for me, even though I promised I would only employ somebody big, fat and ugly."

A few weeks before the marriage, Tim's father took him aside to give him some words of advice. Now retired, Bill Nist was concerned about Tim making Julie a full partner in the business after they married. He warned that it might lead to trouble down the road, and would ultimately be proved right.

"That was a conflict later," says Tim. "She wanted to be in control but she never was when it came to the business. I always had the last say on things whether she liked it or not."

Later, when Julie wanted to be named as a shareholder in the business she had helped to build, Tim adamantly refused, never telling her about his father's warning.

At 2:30 p.m. on Saturday, November 16, 1991, Julie and Tim were married in a Catholic ceremony at St. Gregory the Great Church in Hamilton Square, New Jersey. Viewing it as the most important day of her life so far, the beautiful twenty-three-year-old bride shone like a diamond in her five-thousand-dollar white wedding dress.

The ceremony had to be postponed for almost an hour after Tim left the wedding ring in his car, which was parked where the reception was to be held on the border with Pennsylvania. In the end he had to send a friend to retrieve it. "I kept stalling them until it finally arrived," he remembered.

As Julie walked down the aisle to the strains of the wedding march, her mother burst into tears. Across the church sat her ex-husband John, whom she had not seen outside court for almost fourteen years. Their son John Junior was noticeably absent; he had not been invited.

"I thought she looked *so* beautiful," said her father. "I mean really stunning."

Cheryl Chuplis, as the maid of honor, had helped Julie select her wedding dress a few months earlier. Originally Julie had wanted an ultra-sexy gown to show off her perfect body. But good taste prevailed and she had opted instead for a more conservative, Cinderella-like white lace affair with a long flowing train.

"She said it made her feel like a princess," said Cheryl.

After the ceremony the guests drove to the reception at an Italian night club in Scutters Mill, where Tim had once worked as a disk jockey at weddings. The champagne flowed as nearly a hundred guests feasted on a multi-course meal, prepared to Julie's own demanding specifications.

Julie was anything but a shy, blushing bride when the bar suddenly closed up at 10:00 p.m. Still wearing her wedding gown and flowing train, Julie stormed up to the manager, angrily demanding they re-open it for another hour.

"She got the bar back open," said Tim. "But that's how she was. Julie always got her own way, always."

After the wedding, Tim and Julie spent their honeymoon cruising the Caribbean islands. They were deeply in love. One night on deck they agreed to take at least one cruise a year from then on.

CHAPTER SEVEN

LOVE AND MARRIAGE

If anyone thought that being a wife would slow Julie down, they were mistaken. Always hyperactive, Julie now went into overdrive, adding her new role as wife to her office work and her hectic modeling career.

Tim bought her a sporty new two-door Lincoln Marquis sports car. She would speed from promotion to promotion, charming everybody who met her. To her friends, Julie's life seemed an endless series of projects, and she moved from one to the other without missing a beat.

"Julie was always go, go, go all the time," said Tim. "And I used to say to her, 'You never stop to smell the roses, you never really stop to enjoy what you're doing.'"

Now Julie's number-one priority was finding a spacious new home where they could start married life. She and Tim spent weeks touring prospective properties in some of the best areas of New Jersey, before finally settling for a $218,000 two-story Colonial house in Mansfield Township, fifteen miles south of Trenton.

Originally a rural farming community producing grain crops and beef, Mansfield Township was now coming up in the world, attracting affluent new residents who loved its peaceful rural setting and flat grassland. Midway between Philadelphia and New York, it was the perfect location for up-and-coming businessmen to commute into either city.

While Tim signed the mortgage papers, Julie was in Florida competing unsuccessfully at the national finals of the Miss Hawaiian Tropic contest. In order to raise extra cash for the down payment, he sold his beloved black Porsche.

They moved into their new home in the fall of 1992 and Julie began shopping for furniture. She supervised the conversion of an upstairs room into her office and upgraded the computer system for maximum efficiency.

Now a frequent sight at the *Trentonian* offices, Julie was practically a member of the staff. As the favorite Page 6 model, she now took part in all the promotions, representing the newspaper in the annual round of local parades, charity softball games and other events.

That June she competed in the Swimsuit Contest for the third year running, and came in second, winning $500 and a free trip for two to Jamaica. Julie would win many other local beauty contests, but ironically, she would never crack *The Trentonian*'s, even though readers voted her Page 6 Girl of the Year twice.

Nevertheless, the paper had a special affinity with Julie Nist, as she was now being billed. That summer she made the front page of the annual "Down the Shore" supplement and sensuous bikini shots of her reclining on the beach at Seaside Heights, New Jersey, appeared no fewer than four times inside.

A few weeks later she was summoned to the editor's office late at night regarding a special mission for the newspaper.

"Page 6 was controversial when it came out," Julie said in June 1998, "and Maury Povich wanted to have us on. The night before, I was sitting in the conference room with the editors and they wanted a model who could go on and defend Page 6. Tom Kelly, the Page 6 photographer at the time, recommended me, and everyone went along. I was thrilled they picked me."

Although Julie claimed to have been nervous before the show, she was full of confidence on the set with her show-stopping bikini poses for the audience, producing what she called "a masterful performance."

"I was scared, but my personality kicked in," she said. "And I triumphed."

A few weeks later Julie starred in another segment about Page 6 girls on the then top-rated tabloid TV show *Hard Copy*.

"The newspaper had gotten a call from *Hard Copy* and everything's always last-minute," explained Tom Kelly. "They wanted a couple of models for a video and Julie was picked to be in that. She was pretty natural in that type of thing and it didn't take much for her to get ready. Get out there and do it. That was Julie."

Marriage did not seem to slow Julie down at all. She carried on clubbing and bar-hopping with her girlfriends, while Tim stayed at home watching television or reading.

"Julie loved going out late," said Cheryl Chuplis. "She was always out there [enjoying] her night life, doing this and doing that. She was a great one for that."

Julie and Tim now had different sets of friends and often took separate cars to the same party, in case one of them wanted to move on somewhere else. Friends would remark that the newlyweds seemed distant from each other, often socializing with different people in the same room and displaying little outward affection.

At the beginning of her marriage Julie loved having independence from Tim, who was never jealous of the constant attention she received from men. Later on she would begin to wonder whether he really cared about her.

"I've never seen Julie or Tim really hold hands or kiss in public," said Cheryl Chuplis. "They were never affectionate. More like good friends."

Tim says that Julie was never the kind of extremely physical person who needed to be hugged and kissed all the time. On the other side of the coin he found her very needy and unable to be alone.

"I didn't need to have that social stimulation all the time and Julie did," he explained. "I could be alone and go somewhere by myself and it wouldn't be a problem. She needed me around a lot."

Their once-active sex life had also diminished since they had settled into a domestic routine. "Sex was okay," says Tim. "When it happened it was great. That of course slowed down as it always does in marriage." But they were still in love and would never dream of being unfaithful to one another.

Julie would confide in her mother, saying that Tim often wanted sex when she did not. And although mother and daughter frequently argued, sometimes not talking for days, they were emotionally co-dependent, and told each other everything that happened in their lives.

Julia Scully viewed her new son-in-law as a cold person who looked down on other people. She warned her daughter not to expect too much affection.

"I mean, they were newlyweds and they acted like they'd been married forever," said Julia.

Although Julie's acting career never really took off, in June 1993 she bought an 8mm video camera and began making home movies, recording their lives together on film. One early tape shows Julie spread out on the carpet in her office, happily franking client bills, while she chats to the camera.

"I just got this camera the other day, dude," she tells a friend. "I don't know anything about these things so Tim picked it. The guy who sold it said it was a good one."

Two days later Julie took the camera on a two-day crabbing expedition to the Jersey Shore with a couple of friends. Throughout the trip Julie provided an up-beat commentary on everything that happened, hamming it up for Tim's camera.

"OK, this is me putting my shoes on before we go crabbing," she began playfully, as they prepared to leave from Mansfield Township. The following day on a hired boat, Tim filmed Julie throwing the anchor out and jokingly saying, "No anchor, what'll I do?"

"Once again Julie has been drinking," replies Tim with mock censure.

"Ooooh, party!" she screams later, proudly showing the camera the crabs she's caught and laughingly accusing her husband of being frightened by the creatures.

"Look at our crabs! That's a monster!"

"Julie had a zest for life," Tim would later say. "The early days were such fun. If only they could have lasted."

*   *   *

That fall Julie became a passionate New Jersey Devils ice hockey supporter. Tim had always followed his favorite team around the country and now Julie started attending home and out-of-town games with him, opening up a whole new set of friends for the couple.

In the beginning, Julie stayed at the bar drinking beers and talking while Tim watched the games from his seat, joining her at half-time. Always gregarious, Julie would start a conversation with anyone, genuinely intrigued to find out what made them tick.

At one game that season Julie and Tim met another young supporter named Tony Capella, and they instantly connected. Over the next few years Capella would play an important role in their lives as friend and confidant.

"We became very good friends," said Capella, a successful businessman in his thirties. "We'd go to dinner all the time and I'd go to their parties and they'd come to my beach house to spend time at the beach."

The soft-spoken Capella, who is involved in local Republican politics, would become Julie's mentor, even though he did not approve of her increasingly hedonistic lifestyle.

"She was a partier," he explained. "When you had a gathering of people and Julie showed up, it was a party. And she liked being the center of it. She liked to drink and she was into things that I wasn't necessarily into. I guess she wanted to have fun."

A few weeks later, Tim Nist was in a Trenton sports bar called Champs, watching a New Jersey Devils game on the giant TV. The only other person in the crowded bar wearing a Devils jersey was a young man named Mark Allen. Finding themselves the only two Devils supporters in the bar they started buying each other drinks and discussing the game. They got on so well that they arranged to meet the following week at Champs to watch another game together.

"Mark called me after the game," remembers his girl-friend and now wife, Tracey Buehler. "He told me that he met this neat guy and said, 'We are all meeting next week.' I said, 'Who are *we*?' Mark said, 'Me, Tim, you and Tim's wife, Julie.'"

Mark and Tracey were first to arrive at the bar and were already drinking at a table when Tim and Julie sauntered in.

"I'll never forget the first time I met Julie," said Tracey. "She just walked right up to me and said, 'Yo. I'm Julie! Who are you?' At first her up-frontness threw me. I mean she was right up in my face. No 'Nice to meet you,' or 'Hello, my name is Julie.' That was not her style."

From then on the two couples started meeting regularly to watch hockey games together, either at Champs, or the Sportsman's Pub around the corner. Before long they had become close friends, going to each other's homes to socialize over dinners.

Tracey loved Julie's outgoing, happy-go-lucky personality and they were soon best friends, often attending Devils games at the Brendan Byrne Arena in Newark, New Jersey. The less extroverted Tracey eagerly following Julie's exuberant lead.

"Julie and I would wreak havoc," said Tracey, who was impressed that her new friend seemed to know everyone at the arena. "We'd eat big, fat burgers and really get the whole crowd going. We were both incredibly loud and not afraid of anyone. Our specialty was picking on the opposing teams' fans, especially the Rangers. Julie and I lived to pick on Ranger fans."

Tim and Mark played straight-men to the girls' jibes at rival supporters. When their targets turned to them for support, the two men would merely shrug their shoulders as if to say, 'What do you want us to do?' "

On one occasion Julie wanted to fly with Tracey to an away game in Pittsburgh, but Tim refused to allow it, saying that he didn't have the money to bail them out of jail.

As long as Julie was the center of attention she thrived like a flower in sunlight. But once she was back home alone all her old insecurities would come rushing back. Then she would be looking for the next fix of excitement.

That Christmas, Tim invited Julia Scully to his sister Terry's house for a family celebration. At dinner Tim and Julie seemed the perfect couple, all enigmatic smiles as his family repeatedly asked when they planned to have a baby.

Tim's business was flourishing and the money was rolling in. Julie was now living a life of luxury as the wife of a successful businessman, worlds away from her unhappy, impoverished childhood. Tim was generous, finding it hard to deny Julie anything her heart desired. There were expensive clothes, jewelry and fast cars—she could have everything she had ever dreamed of.

On July 4, 1994, Julie and Tim held a Hawaiian luau at their home for a select group of friends. After a fabulous dinner prepared by Julie, the party retired to the new Jacuzzi that Tim had installed in the garden. As the 8mm camera rolled, an obviously drunken Julie got out of the Jacuzzi, wearing her favorite stars-and-stripes bikini, her fabulous body gleaming in the camera lights.

"Floor show," she spiritedly declared, proceeding to

strike some sexy modeling poses to the applause of her friends. Then she voted her friend Stephen Muster winner of the ugliest tee-shirt contest, and disappeared inside the house to get his prize of Banker's Club Vodka.

Later that night Julie was in her element at the pool table in her basement, vodka in hand, taking on all comers and holding the table.

"I'm mobile," she yelled, lining up shot after shot, clearing the table and winning the game.

Julie held the table for nearly an hour, cracking entertaining one-liners, getting laughs from her guests. The more vodka she drank the better her game seemed to get. That night Julie was unbeatable.

PART TWO

THE PATH TO DESTRUCTION

CHAPTER EIGHT

THE SLIDE

Julie and Tim had always wanted children and around Christmas 1994 they discussed starting a family. Julie was well aware that she would lose her fabulous figure during pregnancy and have to give up modeling, temporarily at least. And now in her late twenties, she was uncertain whether to make the sacrifice.

So she called an old friend named Susan White, who had just become pregnant herself, for advice. Susan had first met Julie almost a decade earlier through her triplet sisters, Ann, Nancy and Carol, all of whom had been friends of Julie's first husband Neal. Eight years older than Julie, Susan had never been as close to Julie as her sisters had been. The telephone call seemed to come out of the blue.

"Julie said she was starting to think about being a mother," said Susan. "And she wasn't sure and was questioning it. I told her there's no real time and when it happens, it happens."

One night Julie was working a Coors Light promotion with Cheryl Chuplis, when she announced she was thinking of retiring from modeling. Then she began to laugh.

"I couldn't believe that came out of Julie's mouth," said Chuplis. "Because she really loved her night life."

Then one night in February 1995, an excited Julie telephoned Cheryl with some news.

"She said, 'Guess what? You're the first one I called because I'm pregnant!' I was, 'Oh my God.'"

Tim was delighted at the prospect of being a father, and Julie's pregnancy drew them closer for a while. She carried on modeling until May, when her contract ran out and she started to show. But she assured clients and friends that she would be returning to modeling, just as soon as the baby was born.

Julie gained thirty-five pounds during her pregnancy and enjoyed displaying her growing tummy at every opportunity. She began to spend more time with her mother, talking about the future and what role Julia would play as a grandmother.

In July, Julie and Tim held their annual summer party, inviting all their friends to the house on Mansfield Road, which was in the middle of renovation. As always Julie was the perfect hostess, holding court on the deck, wearing a one-piece swimsuit and thong.

"She had this big belly," remembers Cheryl, "and she was beautiful, although she was exhausted from trying to do what she did every year."

Although Julie was now forced to cut back on her partying, she continued to drink and smoke throughout pregnancy, refusing to take any criticism from anybody.

"We used to fight all the time about the drinking," remembers Tony Capella. "She drank while she was pregnant, not a lot but she still had her two glasses of wine or whatever her doctor said she could have. She always liked to catch a buzz."

At the beginning of September, Julie, seven months pregnant, went on a camping trip with Tim and several friends. Tim's 8mm camera caught a visibly tired-looking Julie, patting her stomach and declaring, "It won't be long now."

Then she lit up a cigarette by the campfire to the obvious annoyance of Tim.

"That's my wife having a cigarette when she's pregnant," he tells the camera. "The evidence is in her hand."

Then like a disobedient child rebuked by a parent, Julie defiantly waved the cigarette at the camera, turned around, slapped her bottom and asked, "Think my butt is fat?"

The once-skinny model often had a tough time dealing with the changes in her body during pregnancy, and one afternoon she called Tracey Buehler in distress.

"She had the blues," remembers Tracey. "She was feeling big and crass."

During the conversation, Julie mentioned that she had taken a fancy to a golden heart-shaped pendant she had seen in a local jewelry store. As soon as they got off the phone, Tracey called Tim, telling him his wife was depressed and suggesting he buy her the pendant.

"A couple of days later Julie called me," said Tracey. "She said, 'Oh that Tim, he's so sweet. He bought me that heart pendant.' I thought it was so cool and I never told her I had spoken to him."

By the third trimester, Julie was experiencing severe mood swings and her behavior became more unpredictable than ever. That October she attended a New Jersey Devils/Philadelphia Flyers hockey game in Philadelphia with Tony Capella. When another spectator commented on her bulging belly, Julie physically attacked him before an astonished crowd.

"She was eight months pregnant at the time," remembered Capella. "This guy started giving her a hard time and she decked him."

Shortly before she was due, Julie and Tim asked Capella and Mary Jones to be godparents to their new baby. Capella was honored and took Julie and Tim out to a nearby mall to buy a christening gown. Then they went out to dinner to celebrate.

As the birth approached, Julie constantly fielded the inevitable questions from friends about what the baby would be named. One day Julie joked to Tracey Buehler that she planned to name it after the last New Jersey Devil to score before it was born. It became a running gag between the two friends.

One night in late November, Tim Nist called Tracey in the middle of a Devils hockey game, complaining that Julie was cleaning the house like "a madwoman," and that he'd never seen her like this before.

"Oh, Tim, she's nesting," Tracey told him. "You keep an eye on her."

Two hours later an excited Julie called back to announce that her water had broken and they were on their way to Rancocas hospital.

"I'm like, 'No! No! Ricard Pearson was the last Devil to score. You can't name that baby Ricard,' " Tim remembered later, ' "Hold your knees together, girl.' "

As it happened, Julie and Tim named their baby daughter after Scarlett O'Hara, Julie's favorite movie heroine, from *Gone With the Wind*. Katie Scarlet Nist was born on November 26, weighing eight pounds exactly, and pronounced a beautiful, healthy baby by the doctors.

A couple of days later a delighted Julie took Katie home to begin her new life as a mother. She invited all her friends over to see her new baby girl. Everybody agreed that Katie was a lovely baby, speculating that she would inherit her mother's beauty.

A few nights after Katie came home, her father was asleep when Julie came into the bedroom for help, as the baby wouldn't stop crying. "I still have this image of a silhouette of a woman with a crying baby in her arms," said Tim. "I'll never forget it. It was perfect."

That January the East Coast was hit by a record number of blizzards, which paralyzed New York and Philadelphia. Mansfield Township was particularly badly hit during the worst one on January 8th. Massive snow drifts blocked the front door of the Nist house.

While Tim ventured outside into the yard to shovel up the snow that had cut them off from the main road, a radiant Julie nursed Katie by a log fire. Julie's once-troubled life now seemed complete as she tenderly held her new baby daughter up to Tim's camera.

"Six weeks and a day," she proudly announced. "Here you are, Katie, sleepy. Look at her little face. Wow!"

Four days later the snow still lay outside the house as Julie gave Katie her first bath, serenading her with "Old MacDonald Had a Farm."

"Personal grooming is fun, Katie," she told her new daughter.

Motherhood completely changed Julie's life and at first she appeared to take it in stride. She seemed to accept that her freedom would now be curtailed; Katie's welfare had to come first.

Katie was christened on May 19 and Julie would later tell friends it was a wonderful day. Six-month-old Katie cried throughout the service, which was attended by all their friends and family. Katie's proud godparents Mary Jones and Tony Capella took turns in holding her for Tim's 8mm camera.

Soon after she had become pregnant, Julie had called her estranged younger brother John, trying to heal the rift between them. The two Scully children had not spoken in almost five years and in the meantime John had divorced and remarried, and was the father of a second child.

The week after the christening, Julie and Katie flew to Orlando to stay with her brother and his new wife Chelsea. During the trip they went to the Universal Studios theme park, and Julie attended a military ball at the naval base where John was stationed.

Julie was the belle of the ball, dressed in a long black sequin gown and white gloves. At one point she endeared herself to a two-star general by suddenly grabbing him and starting an impromptu conga line.

"We had a really good time," said John. "That's probably the fondest memory I have of my sister. We had got back together again and it was fantastic to have her back in my life."

Back in Mansfield, Julie settled down to her new life as a young mother. It was the slow season for Stirling Lawns, so Julie only needed to do a couple of hours' office work in the afternoons. The rest of the time she took Katie on shopping expeditions and to visit friends.

During this time Julia Scully was a constant visitor to the house, where she often stayed overnight to baby-sit Katie.

"I was there to take care of Katie if Julie wanted to

go anywhere," said Julia. "And for a while she really didn't have any desire to go out."

But Julie and her mother had very different ideas about how to bring up babies, and that would inevitably lead to heated arguments.

"There were times when Julie would kick her mother out of the house for two weeks and not let her come back," said Tony Capella. "I mean, *that* was their relationship."

Julie and Capella both had problems with their mothers, so they developed a special code to signify if they were presently on bad terms with them.

"She would call me and go, 'My mother's making stew!' And I'd know they were having an argument," he laughed.

Over the next two years, Julia Scully's frequent criticisms of her daughter's skills as a mother led to considerable friction. And being a mother herself also resurrected long-suppressed memories of Julie's own miserable childhood.

"I think Katie's birth magnified what [Julie's] parents had done to her," says Tracey. "It really upset her because she looked at Katie and said, 'I love this person so much. How could my father have left me? How could my mother have treated me like that?' I believe she really reflected, which of course everyone does when they have a child. And it hurt her."

That summer Julie sank into a deep depression and took to her bed for days at a time. Her husband and friends tried unsuccessfully to coax her out of the house.

"Julie thought she couldn't go to the Devils games because she had a responsibility to stay home with Katie," said Julia Scully. "I remember Tim saying that he wanted the old Julie back again."

And Julie also confided to her mother that she no longer felt attracted to Tim, having lost all sexual feelings for him. She said all he wanted was sex and it was bothering her more and more.

She was also very self-conscious about her body and was unable to lose the thirty-five extra pounds she had gained during her pregnancy. For the first time in her life Julie was overweight. But she was completely unmotivated to go to the gym and work out, so she could resume her modeling career.

"It was going to take some hard work," agreed Tim Nist. "She said, 'I'm not ready to do that.' And it took some time before she realized that maybe she should."

In the past Julie had always been able to eat anything and never put on any weight. She loved tucking into steaks and burgers and never had to exercise like some models. Now her whole metabolism had changed and it began to take its toll on her, physically and emotionally.

She began to miss the excitement and attention of being a pin-up model.

"Julie liked people to look at her," explained her childhood friend Mary Jones. "She always had to be *the* center of attention and after the baby she became a lot more self-aware of her body. Her figure changed and her waist wasn't as small as it had been. And it bothered her."

That fall, as Julie became more and more frustrated with her life, a friend persuaded her to go into analysis and she began attending weekly sessions. Her psychiatrist diagnosed post-partum depression and prescribed Prozac and tranquilizers. For a while her spirits seemed to rally.

There were fleeting glimpses of the old, fun-loving Julie, but she found it increasingly difficult to balance the demands of motherhood with her love of partying. For the first time in her life Julie felt she was no longer in control.

"I think she felt trapped," says Tim. "She was a party girl and now she couldn't go out like she used to all the time and that was hard for her. Trying to be the old Julie was not going to be that easy anymore."

Tim became concerned that the psychiatrist was forcing Julie to explore parts of her childhood that were best forgotten, causing more problems than he was resolving. As she began to question almost everything in her life, her frequent depressions had a bad effect on her marriage, driving her further away from Tim.

The deeper she went into analysis, the more it highlighted problems in the marriage that had been there all along. "I think there was always a conflict of personalities," says Tim, looking back. "She was not independent and I was. It was always the sticking point for her that I was not giving her the constant reassurance she seemed to want.

"I was not a jealous type and I think that bothered her too. I mean, she could do her modeling and I was always, 'Well, if you go and cheat on me then go ahead ... just don't come home.' "

In April 1997, Tim and Julie went for couples counseling in an attempt to save their ailing marriage. They both wanted to make it work and agreed to lay bare their troubled relationship in front of an impartial counselor.

"There was no argument that we would try it," said Tim. "We had our problems."

But after only a few sessions Julie decided to stop the counseling and concentrate on just seeing her psychiatrist.

"She told me that she couldn't go and see two counselors a week," said Tim. "I think maybe the counselor was getting a little close to finding some of the problems. Julie wasn't ready to try and work it out that way."

A few weeks later Julie told Tracey Buehler about her analyst, surprising her friend by some of the advice he was giving her. Julie said the psychiatrist had told her not to worry if her marriage didn't work out. She was still beautiful and would easily find somebody else to take Tim's place. Being beautiful, she told Julie, wasn't the issue. "I mean was that all she was? But maybe that's all she thought she was, unfortunately," said Tracy.

In April Julie was the matron of honor at Tracey's wedding to Mark Allen. Straight afterwards she took her mother and Katie to Orlando to stay with her brother John and his family. But in Florida Julia noticed how sad and despondent her daughter became whenever she saw John and Chelsea holding hands and being romantic. Julie sadly told her mother that she'd never had that with Tim, as he always wanted his own way and thought she should be interested in his hobbies.

Soon after returning to New Jersey, Julie had dinner with Mary Jones and began discussing the state of her marriage. She said she was going to leave Tim, that her therapist had pointed out she had never been alone and had always had a man in her life.

"She said she wanted to be a single independent woman for once," said Mary.

That summer Julie threw herself into partying with a vengeance. Looking to escape she started going out late into the night with her friends and would often come home drunk. She also began to snort cocaine on weekends for some extra excitement.

In June, Tony Capella invited the Nists, along with a group of his friends, to attend the annual Blue Jean Ball in Newark. It was a glamourous black-tie event for the banking community and every year Capella took a couple of tables to entertain his friends.

Julie arrived exquisitely attired in an evening dress but seemed distracted and bored during the meal. At one point she slipped out of the ball, disappearing for an hour-and-a-half to go into the mean streets of downtown Newark to score some cocaine to liven things up.

"I found out after the fact that she got one of the parking guys to go and find drugs," said Capella, who was hurt by her behavior. "Friends who were at the event told me that's what she did when she was missing."

Julia Scully was also becoming concerned with her daughter's new preoccupation with drugs. One day she was over at their house doing the washing when she discovered a rolled-up twenty-dollar bill in Julie's jeans pocket. Having been around the drug scene herself in the 1960s, Julia immediately suspected her daughter was using cocaine.

At first she decided to keep quiet but when she found a plastic straw in her daughter's trousers a few weeks later, she confronted Julie about it.

"Julie said somebody had some cocaine but it was boring," recounted Julia. "I remember her saying, 'Oh don't worry about it. I only do it occasionally.' I said, 'Yeah, but I've been addicted.' "

Tim Nist claims that he was unaware of Julie's drug use and he never saw any signs. He put her increasingly erratic behavior down to the combination of drinking alcohol and the Prozac, that her psychiatrist had prescribed.

He became convinced that she had lost her bearings

and was floundering. He was staggered by her saying that she didn't feel she deserved her life, and felt it was an ominous sign.

"That's when it changed," he said. "She wasn't herself anymore. I was thinking, 'Wow, if you're not happy here, I don't think you'll ever find happiness.' "

At the beginning of November, Julie suggested to Tim that they take a cruise together to inject some new romance into their relationship. They usually took their annual cruise to the Caribbean in early January but Julie said she wanted to go two months earlier, and then go skiing with friends after Christmas.

Julie went to her travel agent and booked a seven-night cruise aboard Celebrity Cruises' new flagship liner, the Galaxy. The eight-hundred-and-sixty-six-foot cruise ship was the last word in floating luxury, boasting its own casino, nightclub and theater.

Julia agreed to baby-sit Katie while they were away and on Saturday, November 1, Tim and Julie flew to San Juan to join the Galaxy on its first cruise of the winter season.

CHAPTER NINE

THE CRUISE

George Skiadopoulos had always been ambitious, fired with a dogged determination to rise above his humble roots and find success. His father Pavlos was a merchant marine from Athens who moved four hundred miles north to the fishing town of Kavala in the early 1970s, when he met and married a young girl named Simos.

Born on July 24, 1974, George was mostly raised by his mother and grandmother, as Pavlos was often away at sea for long periods at a time. When he came home he would bring his young son gifts from the different countries he had visited, capturing George's imagination with wondrous tales of exotic far-flung places.

As a small boy, George would sneak off through the bustling, narrow alleys of the harbor to watch the big ocean freighters sail away with their cargoes of tobacco and fertilizer. From his earliest days he was fascinated by the sea, dreaming of one day leaving Kavala to follow in his father's footsteps.

Even as a young boy George had two diametrically opposite sides to him. While at school he was a popular, exemplary pupil, who got top grades and never got into trouble, at home he was often impossible, with an uncontrollable temper that could explode into violence. Ironically, the English translation of Skiadopoulos is "son of shadows."

His aunt, Voula Kardasi, would later say that George had shown signs of an unstable personality throughout his childhood. Many family members suspected that George had inherited his mother's schizophrenia, which reportedly had resulted in several spells at a Kavala mental asylum.

Growing up, George had a superiority complex. He was an arrogant loner and mostly kept to himself, having just a few close friends. Although rather plain-looking and small for his age, he had piercing dark eyes with an unnatural power of their own.

"He was a very quiet boy," remembered Demetrios Copsahelios, who grew up in the same Kavala neighborhood as George and was in the same class at St. John's Junior High School. "Nobody ever had any problems with him but he definitely had bigger dreams than the rest of us."

Another school friend, Alexis Makezedis, would describe George as very smart but not the athletic type. "George was the person you would want as a friend," said Makezedis. "He was the best of the best."

In his early teens, George's life changed forever when his father had an affair with a young Turkish woman, soon after Simos had born him a second son. When Pavlos walked out on the family and set up housekeeping in Athens with his girlfriend, George became a pawn in his parents' bitter and often violent divorce.

He would later claim that his father, believing George's mother had taken a lover, had the boy place a bugging device in his mother's house. As an adult he would boast about how he had once climbed a telephone pole to secretly record his mother's conversations with her boyfriend, claiming that he still had the tape in his possession.

After his parents' divorce, fourteen-year-old George went to Athens to live with Pavlos and his mistress. His parents' break-up had a traumatic effect on George, who blamed his father's unfaithfulness for causing it.

One day during an argument George turned violent and stabbed his father in the neck with a kitchen knife, then pushed him down a flight of stairs. Pavlos was hospitalized for a month and remained on medication for years after the incident.

A Greek private detective, who would investigate George ten years later, discovered that after the attack the troubled teenager had been sent to an Athens mental institution and treated with drugs for schizophrenia.

After his release, George returned to his mother in Kavala and resumed his studies at school. He won a coveted place in the nautical high school in Padras and then went on to Salonika to take advanced studies at the Merchant Marines Public School, which he graduated from in 1997.

"I had many family problems because my parents were separated," George would later say. "But despite that I was able to study with patience and persistence and I graduated with good grades."

Pavlos Skiadopoulos, who had reconciled with George after the attack, was delighted that his son wanted to go to sea and used his connections to find him a well-paying job with Celebrity Cruises.

So on November 1, 1997, George joined the Galaxy as third engineer, with special responsibility for maintaining the swimming pool, and was given a smart new naval uniform to wear. Although it was a rather lowly position, he was determined to better himself and move up the naval ladder quickly. After all, he *was* only twenty-three.

There was an air of excitement and expectation among the passengers as they boarded the Galaxy for the first cruise of the winter season. When Tim and Julie Nist arrived they found that the Galaxy was not docked in its usual place in Old San Juan. Instead they had to take a taxi to the ocean liner, where they were escorted to their cabin by immaculately dressed white-gloved Celebrity Cruise stewards.

It was a beautiful hot clear afternoon as the Galaxy slipped its mooring and headed out to sea. The Nists were on deck to watch San Juan recede into the distance. Then they went down to the Oasis Cafe's buffet for a snack, before retiring to their cabin to watch a hockey game on the ship's TV cable system.

Below deck, George Skiadopoulos had been busy working in the engine room, preparing for the seven-day cruise. On his way back to his quarters that night he spotted Julie Nist en route to the casino's slot machines. He was instantly attracted to the beautiful dark-haired brunette in the expensive, low-cut evening gown, and decided she had to be rich because of all the gold jewelry she wore in addition to her huge diamond engagement ring. He made a mental note to try meeting her during the cruise.

That night at dinner, the Nists were delighted to discover they had much in common with the fellow passengers seated at their table. There was a young couple from Detroit, some French Canadians from Ottawa and a husband and wife from Jersey City, New Jersey.

"We met some pretty cool people," said Tim. "You go on some cruises and everyone's a dud, but this one everyone was fun and we hung out together."

The following morning the Galaxy docked at Catalina Island, the cruise line's private port of call in the Dominican Republic. Although it was a beautiful hot day, strong winds whipped up the waves, making it a rough journey ashore on the launches, and causing several passengers to be sick. Once on the beach, Julie stripped down to her bikini and sunbathed alone on an inflatable raft while Tim adjourned to the beach bar with his new friends from Jersey City.

Third engineer George Skiadopoulos had a day off so he headed for the beach with a couple of his crewmates. It was his first free day since he had started his new job and he was glad to be able to relax out of uniform.

As he strolled along the beach he saw Julie Nist lying alone and told his friends he wanted to get to know *the* most beautiful girl on the cruise. Full of macho swagger, he even bet them ten dollars that he would soon have a new cabin mate.

Sitting down next to Julie, he asked her if she was enjoying the cruise, telling her he held a very influential position on the Galaxy. He said this was his maiden voyage and lied that he was twenty-eight years old.

Julie was delighted to meet a crew member, hoping that it could lead to invitations to some of the private cocktail parties that ordinary passengers normally didn't get to go to.

Julie immediately felt comfortable with the smiling Greek and, although he had a thick accent, she liked his exotic charm and easy-going manner. She began to tell him about her life in New Jersey and how she modeled professionally. But when he asked if she was traveling alone, she pointed to Tim at the bar, telling Skiadopoulos that he was her husband.

It wasn't long before Tim saw his wife talking to the sailor and came over to join them, noting that the man was prematurely bald and had bad teeth.

"She said, 'This is George,' " remembered Tim. " 'He works on the ship.' He had a really thick accent and I just said, 'Can you get me to the crew bar?' "

The Greek sailor good-naturedly replied that he could show them the engine room and got up to leave, saying he'd see them around the ship.

By the time they returned to the Galaxy for the black-tie evening meal, Tim had almost forgotten about the third engineer. But Julie was intrigued by the exotic sea-man and was secretly hoping they would meet again.

The following day was spent at sea. That morning Skiadopoulos called the Nists' state room to ask how they were getting on. Over the next few days he would regularly telephone for a chat and they always seemed to be running into him around the ship. When Julie was alone he would stop and talk but if she was with Tim, he would excuse himself, saying he was working.

On Monday, the Galaxy docked in Barbados and Tim and Julie got a taxi into Bridgetown, to a beach next to the Hilton Hotel that they remembered from a previous cruise. They rented some Jet Skis and Julie got into an argument with an islander after she hit a buoy and dented the front of hers.

"This guy and Julie were yelling at each other," said Tim. "So I stepped in and gave him fifty dollars to get him off our backs."

Back on the ship George made a point of asking how their day had gone, offering advice about some of the best attractions aboard. Tim saw him as a non-entity and never perceived anything romantic between him and Julie. But later Skiadopoulos would admit there was "an obvious attraction" between him and Julie from the first moment they met.

During the cruise Julie seemed the happiest she had been in years. In Antigua she got drunk on a "booze cruise" aboard a scaled-down replica of a pirate ship named the Jolly Roger. The next day in St. Thomas they went shopping in the town; Julie bought her mother a gold chain.

"This was probably the most fun Julie and I had had for a long while," said Tim. "It was a great cruise."

On their last night aboard the Galaxy, Skiadopoulos telephoned, inviting Tim and Julie to visit the engine room. During the conversation, Tim asked for his address so they could keep in touch after the cruise was over, but the Greek sailor refused. Instead he suggested they meet him later that evening by the staircase on Deck Five.

When they arrived Skiadopoulos was already there, his dark eyes sweeping furtively around as it was a passenger-only area and forbidden to staff. Leading them down the stairway, he gave them a tour of the engine room and then asked a crewmate to take pictures of them as a memento.

As they were saying good-bye Tim again asked to exchange addresses. Looking embarrassed, Skiadopoulos wrote something down on a card and handed it to Tim. But it was all in Greek.

On Saturday, November 8th, the Galaxy docked in San Juan and Tim and Julie said good-bye to the mysterious Greek sailor. By the time they were boarding the plane back to New York, Tim Nist had already forgotten about him. Julie was strangely silent.

The week after they returned to New Jersey, Julie went to a Devils game with Tony Capella and asked him to meet her in the downstairs bar so they could talk. When he came down, she took him to one side conspiratorially and swore him to secrecy.

"I have to tell you something but you'll have to promise not to tell Tim," she began, a breathless air of excitement in her voice. "I met somebody on the cruise, but nothing happened. But I'm in lust!"

Tony didn't take it too seriously, telling Julie that there was nothing wrong with fantasizing and said it might even help her sex life with Tim.

"That's not the end of the world," Tony told her. "It's not a big deal."

CHAPTER TEN

FALLING IN LOVE

In the weeks leading up to her thirtieth birthday, Julie began to reexamine her life. Regarding thirty as a pivotal landmark, she began telling friends she felt unfulfilled and wished that she had accomplished more. She would briefly mention that she had "met somebody" on the cruise, brushing off any question of it going any further.

From five thousand miles away in his small cabin on the Galaxy, the clever, calculating sailor began to spin his romantic web around Julie. After the cruise Skiadopoulos remained in almost daily contact with her, bombarding her with letters, and telephoning at least once a week. He told her she was beautiful and deserved a man who could appreciate both her beauty and her other qualities. Incredibly, Tim would often answer the phone and speak briefly to George, before putting him over to Julie.

That Christmas Julie was at her most vulnerable. And George did everything right to win her heart, courting her with lavish flattery. She began to reply to his letters

and open her heart to him. She told him her frustrations
with Tim and how she missed the glamour of her old
life in the modeling spotlight.

But unknown to Julie, George was also involved in a
passionate affair with a young Dutch woman who
worked on the Galaxy. Later, when he tried to break off
that relationship, the woman attempted suicide and had
to be transferred to another ship on the Celebrity line.

Now thirteen months old, Katie Nist was a beautiful little
toddler, who had been blessed with her mother's beauty
but was already showing ominous signs of her fiery tem-
perament. She was a friendly girl with long, dark hair
framing a cherubic face, and a big, wide smile.

It was Katie's first real Christmas and Tim wanted to
make it a memorable one. He bought a huge Christmas
tree for the front room and Julie and her mother helped
to trim it.

On December 21, a friend donned a Santa Claus cos-
tume and arrived at the house bearing gifts for Katie.
The little child was entranced by the white-bearded, red-
suited stranger who picked her up with a loud chuckle,
to the obvious delight of her parents.

A home video shows Julie looking bemused and distant as Tim fusses over his little daughter. Wearing a
loose-fitting smock and large horn-rimmed glasses, Julie
is almost unrecognizable from her days as a swimsuit
model.

On Christmas Day, Katie was the center of attention
as Tim opened the many gifts she'd received from
friends and family. The biggest one was a toy kitchen
three times her size, with an ice-making machine, that
dispensed little plastic cubes. She also received a small
bungee frame, to help her learn to walk.

Julia Scully had moved in to care for Katie during the long holiday period and one afternoon they were playing together when Katie suddenly came out with a Greek word. Puzzled, Julia later asked her daughter where Katie could possibly have learned it.

"Then Julie told me she had met a Greek guy," said Julia. "But she said it was nothing and I didn't pay it much attention."

A few days after Christmas Julie had a big fight with her mother, after Julia had criticized her for staying in bed all day. Julia stormed out of the house and back to Philadelphia; it would be weeks before they spoke again.

On January 3, 1998, Tim held a surprise thirtieth-birthday party for Julie. She walked in through the front door to find all her friends lying in wait. For a brief moment Julie seemed back to normal, opening presents and telling everyone how happy she was.

But two weeks later, as they were packing for a skiing vacation with friends, Julie dropped a bombshell. "She suddenly announced we were going on another cruise," said Tim. "I said, 'Where are we going?' and she said, 'On the Galaxy.' I asked her if they were taking a different route this time but she said it was the same one. I said, 'Why do we want to go back to the same stupid islands?'"

Shrugging his shoulders, Tim agreed to a second cruise and a delighted Julie couldn't wait to tell Skiadopoulos the good news.

Throughout Christmas and the New Year Julie had been in daily contact with Skiadopoulos and he had urged her to return to the Galaxy. Julie was desperate to see him once more and find out if it was love between them and if they had a future together.

All through their ski vacation Julie seemed strangely

preoccupied and moody, as if she couldn't wait to come home. "That actually didn't go real well," remembered Tim. "Julie wasn't in the best of moods and I didn't know why, because we were with a lot of friends."

On Friday, February 13, Tim and Julie flew back to San Juan for their second cruise on the Galaxy. As soon as the Nists came aboard, George Skiadopoulos was there to greet them like they were old friends. Still Tim did not suspect that there was anything untoward going on.

As the luxury cruiser retraced its route around the same Caribbean islands, George seemed ever-present, continually calling their state room and making plans to see Julie whenever he could slip away from work.

To Tim, going on the exact same cruise as the one three months earlier was a complete waste of time, and he became more and more bored through the week. He didn't like the people at their table and had little interest in revisiting the same places he had only just been to.

One night Julie and Tim had a big argument after she told him she wanted to go to the disco with George and a couple of girls she'd met on board. Tim told her to go ahead and see Skiadopoulos and then went to sleep.

When Julie met the Greek sailor at the bar, she was upset and started drinking heavily. As she got drunk she began pouring out all her problems with Tim, saying she couldn't see a way out.

Suddenly she became emotional and burst into tears and George invited her back to his cabin so they could talk further. Then, as they lay on his bed, George began telling Julie how beautiful she was and declared his undying love.

When he first tried to kiss her, Julie resisted, saying

she was a married woman and her husband was just a few decks away. But finally she succumbed to his amorous advances and they made love with a desperate passion, an intensity she had never experienced before.

By the time Julie left George to sneak back to her state room a few hours later, she was certain that she was in love. She felt that at long last she had met the man of her dreams, who could love her like nobody ever had before.

As she crept into bed next to her sleeping husband, she went to sleep knowing that she would have to see George again, no matter what it took.

A few days after she returned from the cruise, Julie called her close friends, bursting with excitement. She couldn't wait to tell them that there was a new man in her life, although Tim still had absolutely no idea what was going on behind his back.

"When she told me, I was in shock," said Cheryl Chuplis. "Julie's attitude was like, 'I really like this guy and I got intimate with him.' She gave me an impression like, 'Screw you, Tim, I met somebody else and you're not going to hurt me anymore.' "

Julie also said that she wanted to return to work, and asked Cheryl to line up some modeling assignments for her. In preparation, she joined a local gym and began working out obsessively every day to get back into shape.

Tony Capella found himself in a difficult position when Julie confided that the relationship with Skiadopoulos had turned serious. He was Tim's friend as much as Julie's, and felt very uncomfortable keeping her secrets. Even worse, he was Katie's godfather and he felt a deep responsibility to the child, whom he did not want to see hurt.

"Julie [implied] that they had consummated it," said Capella. "And that's when I said, 'I don't want to know anything.' First and foremost, whatever she was doing to Tim wasn't the problem. It was because she had a baby and whatever else you destroy you had innocent children in the mix. That's where my number one concern was."

Loyal to Tim, Capella now deliberately distanced himself from Julie, whom he felt he no longer knew.

"Everything was *her* happiness, *her* happiness, *her* happiness," he said. "There was a drastic personality change and she wasn't as care-free and happy-go-lucky anymore. Julie was never the kind of person who was very self-oriented but now she was. It was the path of destruction."

Within days of returning to New Jersey, Julie secretly arranged to fly to San Juan so she could spend a night with George, while the Galaxy was moored there. As a cover, she took Katie and her mother to visit her brother John's family in Orlando, just a short flight away from Puerto Rico and George Skiadopoulos.

When Julie told her mother that she had fallen in love with a sailor, Julia tried in vain to talk her out of it. And when her mother asked if she had consummated it, Julie lied and said she had not.

"I told her it was wrong and she had a daughter," remembered Julia. "It was a foolish thing and I told her she would regret it later."

In the weeks leading up to the trip, Tim noticed that Julie was becoming more and more distracted and was losing her focus. Her work began to suffer as she began distancing herself from Tim emotionally, going out of her way to be mean to him.

"George would call now and again," said Tim. "But no more often than he did before."

In the kitchen one day, Tim found a photograph of a bare-chested Skiadopoulos and asked Julie about it. Brushing it off, Julie said that George had given it to her. Then she walked out of the room.

"I thought George was a million miles away on the ship," said Tim. "It didn't interest me."

Julie flew to Orlando with her mother and Katie on March 26, 1998. They spent the day with her brother's family and then the next morning she flew to San Juan and straight into George's arms.

After making love in his cabin all afternoon, they discussed their relationship and planned their next move. As Skiadopoulos held her tight and called her by the Greek version of her name, "Julaki," he swore his undying love.

"We talked seriously about our relationship," he would later recount. "She told me about the problems she was having with her husband and how indifferent he was towards her. She said she was considering a separation."

Skiadopoulos would later maintain that he told her he did not want to be the one to break up the marriage. But according to him, Julie replied that the problems were already there and he was not responsible. As Skiadopoulos tenderly kissed her good-bye and put her in a taxi to the airport, Julie promised to come back and see him as soon as she could get away again.

Back in Orlando, Julie told her brother about George, saying she was in love with him. John refused to condone the relationship, telling her that she would have to live with the consequences.

"It was my sister's life and I supported her either way," he said. "Julie said he made her feel alive and happy and that she wanted to spend all her time with him. He made her feel very attractive and wanted and that's what she was looking for."

After Julie brought Katie back to Mansfield Road she began living a double life. She was now in constant contact with Skiadopoulos, and he became the center of her life, which now revolved around his telephone calls.

She wrote him long, passionate letters covered with big red lipstick kisses. And she began sending him little gifts, even baking him her special cookies. In one love letter she carefully listed her bad habits, like stealing the sheets in bed.

As Julie drew closer to George, she became aloof and hostile to Tim. She began to rebel against him by going on shopping expeditions and running up large bills on his credit cards.

"She'd go out and buy clothes and make-up and whatever," remembered her mother. "When I asked her why, she said it gave her something to do."

Julie was also using more and more cocaine, which was now brought to the house by a friend. Whenever her mother challenged her about drugs, an argument ensued. So she gave up bothering.

That Easter, Julie and Tim had a major quarrel in front of Julia, who could only look on helplessly, knowing her daughter's marriage was coming to an end. But when Julie asked her mother to return to Orlando and baby-sit Katie so she could go to San Juan to see her lover, Julia put her foot down, refusing to abet the affair.

Julie and Tim and their beautiful daughter Katie were a happy family before Greek sailor George Skiadopoulos entered their lives. (Photo courtesy of Tim Nist)

George Skiadopoulos in the engine room on the Galaxy where he worked as a third engineer. (Photo courtesy of Tim Nist)

Even at three, Julie Scully knew she had star quality.
(Photo courtesy of Julia Scully)

Julie fell head-over-heels in love with Tim Nist when they first met at Bordentown Yacht Club in July 1989. (Photo courtesy of Tim Nist)

Julie was the most popular Page 6 Girl in *The Trentonian* and starred in many promotions for the newspaper. (Photo courtesy of Tom Kelly)

Tim Nist's photo of Julie which launched her on a successful modeling career after they sent it to *The Trentonian*. (Photo courtesy of Tim Nist)

During her modeling days Julie met many celebrities, including TV game show host Bob Barker. (Photo courtesy of Tim Nist)

The fabulous colonial house in Mansfield Township where Julie and Tim Nist lived even had a Jacuzzi in the garden. After the Nists divorced, Skiadopoulos would spend time there with Julie. (Photo courtesy of John Glatt)

Julie and her daughter Katie both loved going to the beach where they shared some of their happiest times together. (Photo courtesy of Tim Nist)

The Celebrity Cruise ship, the Galaxy, where Julie met George Skiadopoulos for the first time and fell in love. (Photo courtesy of Tim Nist)

Julie's husband Tim took this picture of Greek sailor George Skiadopoulos, soon after they met him aboard the Galaxy. (Photo courtesy of Tim Nist)

To: Georgie Skiadopoulos
    Extension: 7816
    Cabin: 33X3

From: Julie Skiadopoulou

Hi Honey!

It's 1:25 and Katie and I haven't left yet, so I wanted to let you know that I won't be back until after dinner, maybe around 8:00 p.m. I don't want my honey to worry about me. So I'll fax you later to let you know how my day was. 6dex?

I hope you have a nice day, sweetie.

From your moraki.....

Julie

P.S. I Love you.
P.P.S. I miss you.
P.P.P.S. I LOVE YOU!!!!!!
P.P.P.P.S. I need your lovin'.
P.P.P.P.P.S. I want you!
P.P.P.P.P.P.S. Now, today and forever!

PPPPPPS Susan just called Robbie might have the chicken pox! So, she's taking him to the doctor We might still go to the amusement park I'll let you know what happens.
                    I love my Georgie!

One of the dozens of love letters that Julie faxed Skiadopoulos aboard the Galaxy during the torrid affair. (Courtesy of Tim Nist)

Julie exchanged engagement rings with George Skiadopoulos at her 31st birthday party in Kavala on January 3, 1999. Five days later he would murder her in a jealous rage and cut off her head. It has never been found. (Photo courtesy of Tim Nist)

The McDonald's in Omonia Square, Athens, from which Skiadopoulos claimed Julie had disappeared. (Photo courtesy of John Glatt)

Tim Nist brought Julie's remains home to New Jersey and held a moving memorial service for her at St. Andrew's Roman Catholic Church in Jobstown, where their daughter Katie had been baptized. (Photo courtesy of John Glatt)

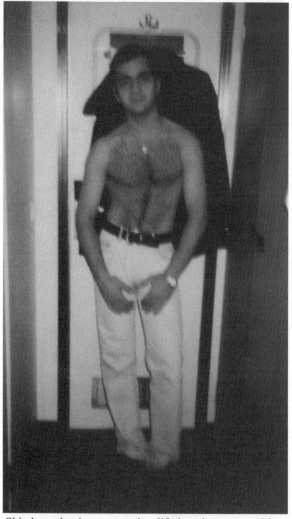

Skiadopoulos is now serving life imprisonment without parole for the inhuman murder of Julie Scully.
(Photo courtesy of Tim Nist)

"I said I was not going to be a party to it," said Julia. "I wouldn't go."

Julie was heartbroken that she wouldn't be able to see Skiadopoulos, and poured out her loneliness in her letters to him. She wrote that she was scared of being alone and felt terribly insecure.

She would spend hours in her office looking up his hometown of Kavala on the internet, day-dreaming of meeting his friends and family. When he eventually invited her to spend two weeks with him in his cabin during an upcoming Galaxy cruise to Alaska, she happily agreed.

On May 15, George wrote a love letter to Julie that revealed just how far their relationship had come in the three months since it had been consummated. Calling her "sweetheart" and declaring his undying love, he wrote glowingly about their future together with Katie.

"You are my life," he gushed. "I love you from the bottom of my heart."

He then asked Julie to send him a sexy video of herself as soon as possible, as he now had access to an 8mm video camera. His other good news was that he now had a new cabin to himself so they could enjoy total privacy when she soon came to visit.

"Don't worry my love," George reassured her. "I'm here for you. Maybe it sounds stupid, crazy and nobody can believe that, but who knows the truth? I DO, I LOVE YOU."

Signing it from "Your macho-baby man", he drew hearts and kisses all over the letter like a smitten schoolboy.

At the end of May, Tim Nist flew to Ottawa with Tony Capella for an important New Jersey Devils play-off game. On the flight back, Tim asked Capella what was happening to Julie, placing him in a difficult position.

"He was pretty quiet about it," said Tim. "Maybe he saw problems, but he told me that he hadn't really talked to Julie."

On his return to New Jersey, Tim persuaded Julie to go back into marriage counseling one last time. After nearly seven years of marriage the couple was constantly fighting, and Tim still had no suspicions that Julie was in love with another man.

At the first counseling session Julie suddenly announced that she wanted a separation and Tim upped the stakes by declaring that he wanted a divorce.

Remembered Tim: "And then the counselor said to me, 'Why are you looking at things in black-and-white?' I said my switch is either on or off. If she wants to go, let her go."

Tim and Julie agreed that he would move out, as it would be better for Katie to remain with her mother in familiar surroundings. "That's great," said Tim. "She wants to separate and I've got to leave the house."

CHAPTER ELEVEN

CLOSING THE DOOR

At the beginning of June, Tim found a bachelor apartment in Hamilton Township and moved out of the Mansfield Road house. He stopped all their joint credit cards, telling Julie she was now responsible for her personal bills. He agreed to pay the mortgage, heating and electricity, but Julie had to pay for everything else including the swimming pool.

Katie was still too young to understand that her parents were splitting up, and as Julie was still running Stirling Lawns' office from the house, Tim came around almost every day on business, so the child hardly noticed any difference.

As Julia Scully moved in to help look after her granddaughter, Julie prepared to fly to Vancouver and spend two weeks with Skiadopoulos on the Galaxy. She told Tim that she was going on a retreat in Michigan with her masseuse.

"She lived, breathed and ate for George," said Tracey

Buehler. "If he was going to call her at 10:00 p.m. she had to be there. Everything was about George."

Like a love-struck teenager, Skiadopoulos wrote long, rambling letters declaring his love for Julie. Now with Tim out of the way, the Greek sailor insinuated himself even further into her life, urging her and Katie to move to Greece so they could all start a new life together.

But Julie still had reservations about walking out on her affluent life in New Jersey, wanting to get to know Skiadopoulos better before she fully committed herself.

"I don't misunderstand that you're hesitant about moving right away to Greece," wrote Skiadopoulos, adding that he was willing to break his contract with Celebrity Cruises so he could take care of her. "I completely understand the reasons. Don't worry."

By now he had come clean and admitted that he had initially lied about his age and was only twenty-three. He excused himself, saying he feared she would think him too young. Julie did worry that he wasn't mature enough to be a proper father to Katie. But in his letters, Skiadopoulos always succeeded in overcoming her reservations with a combination of stroking her ego and cleverly relating to whatever she was going through.

Julie's friends still believed that she would soon come to her senses and return to Tim after she had had a taste of freedom and independence. But George now began a campaign to make Julie wholly dependent on him and she was too vulnerable and weak to see through him.

Wrote Skiadopoulos: "People sometimes become unsure of themselves and their capabilities when they have to make a decision or take a risk that has to do with their future. But I do believe that there isn't any meaning in this life without a risk and sometimes you don't have to think but feel."

During this difficult period, Julie's friends rallied around to support her. Although none approved of her leaving Tim for a stranger she had met on a cruise, they rarely reproached her and tried their best to be understanding. Besides, everyone knew that once Julie had made up her mind to do something, it was impossible to change it.

The last person to know about the affair was Tracey Allen. Julie knew Tracey would disapprove because of her strong religious beliefs and only told her in May, after she had agreed to separate from Tim.

"I don't think Julie ever would have broken up with Tim if there wasn't somebody whispering in her ear," said Tracey.

When Tim moved out, Julie found a lawyer to negotiate her divorce settlement. During their marriage, Stirling Lawns had made Tim a millionaire, and now Julie wanted her share. She began looking for a new house with her mother in some of the most desirable areas of South Jersey.

"At that point I don't think she was one hundred percent committed to George," said her mother. "This was just some guy she had met and she wanted to see him again."

But as George's letters and telephone calls continued, he gradually won her over and she began to consider the possibility of moving to Greece so they could be together. A few days before she left for Vancouver, she stunned her mother by telling her about her new plan to move to Greece with Katie.

"I was very upset," said Julia. "I said, 'Katie will be like a stranger there.' She told me I could come and stay with them whenever I wanted. That's when I knew she had already made up her mind and once she gets that way there's nothing you can do."

A week before she flew to Vancouver, Julie got a call from a *Trentonian* reporter named Eric Ladley, requesting an interview for a "Where Are They Now?" series that he was writing on former Page 6 girls. The tabloid, which under new management had toned down its act, was now reintroducing its monthly beauty competition.

When Ladley arrived at Mansfield Road, Julie seemed up-beat, telling him that she planned to resume her modeling career as soon as she returned from "a secret vacation." When Ladley asked her where she was going, Julie coyly refused to elaborate, saying: "When I get back, I'll be tan, rested and ready, just like Richard Nixon."

During the ninety-minute interview, Julie continually complained to Ladley that she had gained weight and had not been able to model. But she pledged to lose several pounds while she was away.

At one point Tim Nist came downstairs from his office, angrily waving a telephone bill and they got into a heated argument in front of the reporter. Later, when she had calmed down, Julie told Ladley about her ambitious plans to start an exercise regimen so she could resume modeling. She also planned to start night classes at a local community college and study chemical engineering, in case her modeling career didn't work out.

"It seemed like she was grasping for straws," said Ladley. "She seemed depressed that she wasn't modeling anymore and didn't like the way her life was now."

Towards the end of the interview Julie went off the record, confiding to the reporter that she was planning to visit Greece later in the year. Surprised, Ladley asked her if she was going for the cultural or historical attractions. Julie laughed, saying she was going to hang out and get a sun tan.

The two-page feature on Julie appeared on June 15, and an old 1992 bikini shot of her graced the front page. Headlined "Six Appeal! The models who made the page after 5 famous," Julie was described as a "model employee."

In the story, which noted that she was divorcing Tim, Julie sounded like a retired politician on the stump, trying to make a comeback.

"I was proud to be associated with the Trenton area and representing it on Page 6," she was quoted as saying, adding that she was considering changing her license plates to "PAGE 6."

"It's a great conversation opener. Women even come up to me and tell me that their husbands clipped my picture out."

This would be the last time that Julie would ever appear on the front page of *The Trentonian* during her lifetime.

On June 19, Julie flew to Vancouver and joined George Skiadopoulos on the Galaxy. He had told his superiors and shipmates that Julie was his fiancée, so she would be allowed to stay in his cabin. For her third voyage aboard the Galaxy, Julie would share the meager staff quarters and would not be able to use the luxurious restaurants and casinos as she had done with Tim. But all this added to the romance for Julie, who assured the third engineer that she had no problems at all "slumming it."

At his request, she had brought a selection of sexy black lingerie and high-heeled shoes. When she stepped off the plane in Vancouver into bright sunshine, she was full of excitement at the prospect of seeing her lover again. After meeting her at the Canada Place Terminal and escorting her onboard, George had to go to work in the engine room. The Galaxy departed for Alaska two-and-a-half hours late at 8:00 p.m.

For the next two weeks Julie and Skiadopoulos were inseparable whenever he wasn't working. He was even more loving and attentive than she remembered. Every night they would retire to his tiny cabin and make love, experimenting with new positions and accessories like champagne and chocolate sauce.

To Julie it was as if they were *the* only ones aboard their own personal Love Boat. Photographs of the couple from the cruise show them gazing dreamily into each other's eyes on deck as the sun set dramatically behind them. As the Galaxy sailed past Ketchikan and Skagway and rounded the spectacular Hubbard Glacier in Alaska, she fell even deeper under George's romantic spell.

As they began to plan a new life together in Greece with Katie, they spent many hours talking about their lives and dreams. Julie told George about her miserable childhood, which in many ways mirrored Skiadopoulos's own. As children of divorced parents they both related to each other's experiences, deciding they were soul-mates.

One night Skiadopoulos confessed the affair with the Dutch girl, saying that he had ended it when he met Julie and acknowledging that she had attempted suicide. Although it would later come to haunt her, George spun the affair so well that *he* emerged as the injured party. Julie immediately forgave him.

When she was with George, Julie forgot all her problems back home and stepped into a world of the heart and senses that bore little relation to reality. "We lived in intense happiness," Skiadopoulos would later say of his relationship with Julie. "Our love affair progressed into a great passion."

One afternoon, George told Julie that early next year he would have to serve his compulsory two-year military service in the Greek Army. With tears in his eyes he said he didn't want them ever to be apart and that he would do anything to avoid going.

They discussed his fleeing to the United States to avoid the army, and Julie promised to use her connections to explore how he could get a green card. Then they pledged never to leave each other, no matter what it took.

Before Julie left, they agreed he should come and stay with her in New Jersey just as soon as he could get the necessary visas. In these two weeks their relationship had moved forward a quantum leap, and Julie promised: "Just know that I will do everything I can to clean up all the details of my life so we can close the door."

Julie landed at Newark Airport a little after midnight on Saturday, July 4. She was met by Susan White, who drove her back to Mansfield Township, where she arrived at 3:30 a.m. Katie rushed downstairs to greet her mother, whom she had missed terribly.

After grabbing a few hours' sleep, Julie asked Susan to take Katie swimming in the garden, while she went upstairs to her office to send a fax to Skiadopoulos.

"I can't live without you," she wrote. "Nothing will make me feel happy or satisfied until we are together permanently. I can feel the stress taking over and the tears coming because I miss you terribly. I need you with me. I feel like a part of me has been taken away."

Since the second cruise, Julie had grown far closer to

Susan White, who now spent most of her free time at Mansfield Road with her son Robbie, Katie's favorite playmate. Julie and Sue were now together so often that there were rumors that they had become lesbians, which they both found hilarious.

"Ha! if only they knew but they will soon," wrote Julie to Skiadopoulos. "Susan's husband almost punched the guy that started it but [she] stopped him. Isn't it funny?"

Julie felt Susan was the one friend who never criticized her for loving Skiadopoulos, the one friend who could empathize. She told Sue all about her "secret" vacation with George, saying that she was "numb" without him. It had been, she explained, "the most incredible two weeks of [my] entire life."

The only thing Julie had missed while she was away was Katie, who was growing up into a beautiful little girl with a strong will of her own.

"Katie is really different," Julie wrote George. "[She] seems so grown up. Wait 'til you meet her. She is sooooo pretty. Her hair is up right now (just like mine)."

Within hours of coming home, Julie began feuding with her mother. "Well, it's started already," Julie wrote Skiadopoulos. "An argument—just this minute. My mother wants me to call my brother. I told her that I will as soon as I finish this letter to you. She said she thinks my brother is more important." His seven-year-old son Joel had just been diagnosed with a rare blood disease. "I just told her NO, that you are more important and she went in her room and slammed the door. GET USED TO IT MOM."

As soon as George received the fax in Cabin 3383 he replied, telling Julie that she could never imagine how much he loved her. Full of concern for Katie, he asked how she was, saying he couldn't wait to meet her. Calling her by his pet names of "Julaki" and "Moraki," Skiadopoulos finished the fax by saying, "Please take care of yourself and Katie."

Over the next two months Julie and George faxed each other obsessively, up to five times a day. Julie's mother was frequently woken up by the sound of the fax machine going off at three in the morning, leading to even more arguments when she asked her daughter to turn it off so she could sleep.

Julie ran up thousands of dollars' worth of fax and telephone bills to the Galaxy, which she duly charged to Stirling Lawns. Whenever Skiadopoulos was off duty they would talk late into the night.

"Between the sheets, that's where I'd like to be right now, with you," Julie wrote. "In our cabin, in our bed or on the moon. I don't care, as long as my Georgie is next to me."

In another fax Julie teased, "Hi there Sexy! Guess what I did after we hung up the telephone. Sweet Dreams!"

As they had cruised Alaska, Julie had told Skiadopoulos that she was in analysis and was taking Prozac and other prescribed drugs. George told her he was against drugs and persuaded her to throw them away and not take any more. She dutifully obeyed. Without the tranquilizers to calm her down, her mood swings became more pronounced.

"George just made her quit it cold turkey," said Tracey. "It really scared me. But I think that was all part of his game to control her."

Ironically, Julie now began partying harder than ever, often drinking liquor and snorting cocaine late into the night. She and her friends frequently played pool and listened to rock music to all hours, as little Katie roamed freely through the house.

"I'd know the minute she did cocaine," said her mother. "Somebody would come and visit her and her mood would suddenly change. I would be woken up at one in the morning and the kids are running through the house. She must have thought I was stupid, but I knew."

Julie was secretive about her increasing substance abuse. She told few friends and never discussed it with Skiadopoulos, as he would not have approved.

One night her mother was so upset she couldn't sleep so Julie gave her the prescription for the sleeping pills that Skiadopoulos had forbidden her to take.

"I went to the drug store and got the sleeping pills and two refills," remembered Julia. "After that her friends would always ask me for pills late at night."

Julie had also become addicted to her strenuous daily work-outs in a local gym. Determined to return to modeling she embarked on an obsessive exercise regime, spending over two hours a day on machines, doing hundreds of situp's and walking for miles.

Soon she had shed twenty pounds and in mid-July, Cheryl Chuplis arranged for her to do an in-store promotion for Captain Morgan Rum at $25 an hour. Julie faxed the news to Skiadopoulos, explaining that it was "Very innocent!" as it was not in a bar or a club. Within an hour he faxed her back, forbidding her to do it. Without argument, Julie called Cheryl and canceled.

"I would book her for jobs with me and she would cancel at the last minute," said Cheryl. "And I started getting a little frustrated."

When Cheryl asked her friend why she was acting so

unprofessionally, Julie replied that George did not want her to show off her body to other men.

"That's what really triggered stuff and I was floored," said Cheryl. "I said, 'Julie, what are you talking about? This guy's on a cruise ship and you're worried about what he thinks you're doing? Tim never stopped you doing this. I can't believe you're letting him tell you what to do.' "

The Trentonian also made several appointments for Julie to do her comeback Page 6 spread, but each time she backed out at the last minute.

When Tracey heard over the phone that Skiadopoulos had forbidden Julie to model, she got into a big fight with Julie, ending when Tracey hung up on her. They soon made up and Allen learned never, ever to criticize George.

"She was such an emotional yo-yo," said Tracey. "I knew that she was having emotional problems but I decided I was going to stick with her as she was going to need me one day."

Whereas the old Julie was stubborn and headstrong and went her own way, she now seemed hopelessly under Skiadopoulos's control. He seemed to have become her Svengali, as he became even more possessive, methodically distancing her from old friends, who felt they no longer knew her.

"He was ruling everything she did," said Chuplis. "But in a way I think Julie liked it because she thought it was him caring. She took his jealousy to be a sign he really loved her, because Tim never showed a jealous side."

On July 16, Tim Nist arrived at the Mansfield Road house to work on his payroll, only to find himself locked

out. Julie had left with Katie to buy a birthday present
for George, putting a handwritten sign on the front door,
saying, "Do Not Enter!" Tim was livid, realizing that
Julie's behavior was now a direct threat to his business.
So he put his own note on the door, saying he'd return
the following day.

Things had begun escalating a couple of days earlier,
when Julie and her lawyer met with Tim to discuss her
settlement and could not agree on a figure.

"Tim is trying to piss me off (as usual) with the settlement," she wrote to George. "But he isn't succeeding
which probably makes him more frustrated! Oh well!!
I'm making copies of tax records right now so I can give
them to my lawyer. The Big 'A' is coming here tomor-
row."

She also told Skiadopoulos that she had saved Tim's
note in case she had to file harassment charges against
him later. Next time she pledged to leave a drawing of
a skull and crossbones, with the warning, "Enter at your
own risk!"

Fearing that Julie might try to sabotage his business
out of sheer spite, Tim decided to transfer the office to
a nearby warehouse he owned, instructing his employees
to turn up early the next day to help him move. Sensing
trouble from Julie, he also alerted the local police, who
told him there was no law to prevent him from entering
the house to transfer his office.

At 7:00 a.m. the next morning Tim and his men
pulled into the driveway in a large moving van. Julie
saw them approaching the front door and came out to
ask Tim what he was doing. When Tim replied that he
was moving the office out, Julie started screaming at
him.

"I said you can either allow me inside or we'll do it

the hard way," said Tim. "And she said 'No.' So I called the police and said, 'We have a problem.' "

Within minutes five New Jersey state trooper cars had arrived. When a policeman knocked on the door, Julie yelled out that no one was going to get in the house.

"She almost got arrested," said Tim. "She was throwing such a fit."

Finally Julie's attorney arrived and calmed her down, persuading her to allow Tim to go through with the move. Even as his men were carrying out the files, Tim assured Julie that she could stay on as his office manager, working from the warehouse, and still draw her paycheck.

After the confrontation, Julie became paranoid, fully convinced that Tim was spying on her. Sensing an opportunity to distance her even further from her friends, Skiadopoulos added fuel to the fire, warning her to watch out for "the Big 'A.' "

Julie became delusional. She accused her mother and some of her closest friends of spying on her for Tim. "I got really upset," said Sue White, whom Julie accused of taking money from Tim. "And I stormed out crying. I was so pissed at her." The following day Julie called Sue and apologized for her behavior.

As summer wore on, Julie turned her back on the real world, and retreated into the carefully constructed romantic paradise cultivated by George Skiadopoulos.

"I am swimming in a sea of your love," she wrote him. "I'm not afraid to drown. I'm breathing in everything."

She told him that she no longer wanted to go out of the house as it means being "distracted by other things and that means I can't think about you as much."

She sent him romantic lyrics from Elton John's "The

One" as well as several of her favorite Lionel Richie songs, sharing the soundtrack she had selected for their relationship. In the corners of her faxes she drew large hearts pierced by arrows saying, "Julaki loves Georgie" and covered them in lipstick smears from her perfect lips.

"I want your body," she wrote. "I can't bear to be without you. Thank you for everything you did today to make me feel better. It worked. You really do understand what 'makes me tick' and you know just what to say to make me love you even more than I thought possible . . . Like I said—I LOVE YOU MORE TODAY THAN YESTERDAY. BUT NOT AS MUCH AS TOMOR-ROW!!"

CHAPTER TWELVE

BLIND PASSION

In mid-July, Julie became secretly engaged to George Skiadopoulos. Although Tim remained unaware of the affair, she began preparing to move to Greece early in the New Year with Katie, who would be a bridesmaid at their wedding.

She began referring to the Greek sailor as "my future husband"; he announced grandiose plans to buy her a costly engagement ring and to have a traditional Greek wedding in Kavala that would please his family.

"Sweetie, maybe you should reconsider the ring," Julie wrote him on July 18. "I think you should save the money. Really I would be happy with a simple one. *One that matches yours.* I don't need such an expensive ring to remind me of our love."

In the end he sent her an inexpensive gold ring with two dolphins framing a gemstone. Though it looked out of place next to her other, more expensive jewelry, she proudly displayed it to her friends.

Julie was in the final stages of planning a second visit to Vancouver to see Skiadopoulos when he told her not to come. Instead, he said, he would break his contract with the Galaxy and come and see her. He added that a fellow shipmate had promised to forge the necessary paperwork for him to illegally enter the United States as a student.

Now fully absorbed with George's upcoming twenty-fourth birthday on July 22, Julie prepared a special care package for him. It included an English/Greek dictionary, the "best" razor she could find for "that gorgeous face of yours," and an Elton John CD, so he could listen to her favorite tracks, which she carefully marked.

Julie had begun attracting attention at the Trenton Post Office. with her succession of brightly-wrapped parcels addressed to the Galaxy. Several curious postal workers asked who the lucky recipient was.

"It worries me a little that they seem to talk about me and my mail [between themselves]," she complained in a fax to Skiadopoulos. "I guess their lives are boring or maybe they have nothing better to do than talk about me. They probably read the newspaper article about me. *Everyone* says hi to me now whenever I go into town to the store, bank, post office etc. Being famous can have its disadvantages, I guess!! Oh well."

Although Julie strove to be a good mother, she gave Katie total freedom and found it increasingly hard to control her. Now almost three years old, the little girl was mainly looked after by her grandmother and spent her time alternating between Mansfield Road and Tim Nist's new apartment in nearby Hamilton. Since her parents' break-up Katie had started to rebel.

"We're having a disagreement at the moment," Julie faxed Skiadopoulos. "[Katie] wouldn't eat her dinner so

I told her—no TV and that she had to sit on her sofa until she ate. Now, she won't speak to me or look at me. And she's still sitting there. It's been about twenty minutes.

"I have a feeling she is going to be stubborn. I have no idea where she gets that trait from. Ha-ha! The apple doesn't fall far from the tree."

After her own abusive childhood, Julie felt uncomfortable punishing Katie when she was naughty. She remembered only too well how her own mother had beaten her, and she was afraid of being too harsh.

"George, you know, I'm not that good at disciplining Katie," she wrote. "She just dumped beads all over the kitchen floor and won't pick them up. Sometimes I have to raise my voice with her so she knows I'm *serious*. But she still ignores me. I just asked her again if she wants to pick the beads up and she said, 'No, mom' and pointed her finger at me. So, now no Pooh Bear, Binky (pacifier) or TV until she does.

"It would be a lot easier and a lot less stressful if I picked them up. But, if I do, then she'll think she can always 'get her way'. So now I'm 'Mad Mamma' as she calls me when I discipline her! Help!"

A couple of days later Skiadopoulos, who had taken to referring to Katie as "our daughter," wrote that he knew a good way to discipline her, outlining his simplistic views on bringing up children.

"You will see when we go to Greece how much my brother and my sister love me and also respect me. I think it is very important to make the person understand that he or she will lose your love if they do the 'wrong things.' "

Skiadopoulos said it would take "hours to explain"

his child-rearing theories, but promised to do so when the time was right.

Towards the end of July, Tim Nist received a seven-thousand-dollar phone bill for satellite telephone calls and faxes to the Galaxy. He immediately called Julie's mother, asking what she knew about it. Now Julia had no alternative but to tell Tim the truth about her daughter's affair with George, and how she had cheated on him before their separation.

"There was some hurt there," admitted Tim. "*I* had never been unfaithful. But I knew our marriage was over. I basically said, 'Fine—if that's what she wants then hurry up and get it over with.' "

Now that everything was out in the open, Julie started implementing plans for her and Katie to move to Greece and set up house with Skiadopoulos. When she told her mother and some close friends what she proposed, they were dumbfounded. But once again they acquiesced, knowing it was impossible to talk Julie out of something once she had made a decision.

"A lot of people just stopped talking to her because of the way she was acting," remembered Tracey Buehler. "And she also closed herself off to a lot of her friends. I myself told Julie, 'Oh, whatever makes you happy.' "

On July 21, Julie met with her attorney and began preparing for a custody battle with Tim should he try to prevent her taking Katie to Greece. She instructed her lawyer to write to Tim's attorney, outlining her future plans, offering him two months' visitation with Katie each summer.

"I will finally know where I stand with the Big 'A' and what his reaction is going to be," she wrote Skiadopoulos. "I know it will not be good."

Julie even considered taking out a restraining order against Tim, in case he tried to take Katie away from her, but rejected Skiadopoulos's suggestion that she just run away to Greece with her child anyway.

"I am so apprehensive of what the Big 'A' is going to do," she wrote. "But it has to be this way. I can't just leave and take Katie. First of all it's illegal and I will be in trouble with the court."

Manipulating Julie from his cabin at sea, Skiadopoulos now advised her on almost every aspect of her life. But she ignored his advice when she told her mother about taking Katie to Greece. Julia, who was drinking when she heard, desperately tried to reason with her daughter, telling her that she might be in love but it was wrong to take Katie away from her home to a small town in the wilds of Greece.

"Now she is drunk and I can't stand being around her," faxed Julie to Skiadopoulos after the conversation. "It makes me nauseous. I don't know what I expected [my mother] to do or how she would react from being separated from Katie. I should have known. I refuse to let it affect me because my decision is made. I told her to stop living through me and get on with her own life."

Ordering her mother never to bring up the subject again, Julie said they must enjoy the little time they had together before she left.

"Of course, she changed the subject and started arguing about something else," Julie wrote. "I *refuse* to be drawn into an argument. No more. Never. I have been fooling myself about how easy it would be to finish all these details. But I need to get started and *now* I have."

Julie then gave Skiadopoulos the "good news" that he could come and visit her in New Jersey, as soon as he could break his contract with Celebrity Cruises.

"The sooner the better. I need you here. With me."

That day Skiadopoulos submitted his resignation, effective August 28. His chief officer summoned him to his office to try and talk him out of it, but George was adamant, saying that he was getting married.

He faxed Julie to "calm down," telling her not to worry as he would be beside her very soon.

In spite of everything, Julie continued working for Stirling Lawns from her new office in the company warehouse. Although Tim did his best to maintain a friendly business relationship with his estranged wife, her heart was no longer in the job.

Most days she would get up and make Katie breakfast before going to the gym at 9:00 a.m. for a two-hour work-out. She would then stroll into the warehouse around midday and stay for a couple of hours before going home to call Skiadopoulos and prepare to move to Greece.

At night she would wait by the telephone for calls from Skiadopoulos or write him suggestive faxes about the treats awaiting him when he came to stay. She promised romantic bubble baths in her Jacuzzi with strawberries, chocolate syrup and champagne.

"Then you can wash my hair and I'll wash your entire body. How about a massage afterwards with some scented massage oil? Give me your opinion and/or suggestions . . ."

In early August, Julie took Katie to the Jersey Shore to spend the weekend at Tony Capella's beach house. When they arrived, there were no signs of Capella, so they headed for the beach where he eventually caught up with them.

As Katie happily played by herself in the sand, Julie told Capella about moving to Greece and marrying Skiadopoulos. She said she hoped to bring George to the shore to meet Tony, when he came to New Jersey.

But Katie's godfather, ever-loyal to Tim, wanted nothing to do with Skiadopoulos.

"I remember saying to Julie on the beach that day, 'You know if you go [to Greece] we'll probably never see you again,'" Capella remembered. "My feeling was that if she didn't get her life under control, whether it was the drugs or whatever, she would probably wind up gone."

Julie laughed it off, telling him not to worry as she was a winner and always landed on her feet.

"She had that false bravado," he said. "She thought she was invulnerable."

In the days leading up to George Skiadopoulos's arrival, all the stress of the last few months began to take its toll on Julie. When her long dark hair began falling out by the handful, she saw a doctor, who diagnosed an overactive thyroid, a condition she'd suffered from two years earlier.

Her whole life revolved around George and their future. She couldn't sleep and had constant headaches and a bad stomach.

"I can't live like this," she complained. "I am so sad. I don't know what to do."

The unhappier she became the more she worked out, sometimes going to the gym twice a day. Often Tim would be there doing his exercises and she would ignore him. They were now arguing through their attorneys about everything, down to Julie's bottled water and whether it was a company expense.

"I'm thinking about maybe going back to the gym," she wrote Skiadopoulos one afternoon. "I'm not sure that I should because maybe I'll strain myself. My abs already hurt from doing so many sit-ups. But you know what they say—No pain, no gain!"

Julie's behavior was becoming more and more irrational: she escaped into excessive work-outs during the day, and drugs and alcohol at night. Her work was suffering and her mother often helped her prepare client statements at home, so the checks would come in on time to make payroll.

When Julie announced that she could no longer go to the warehouse because the "pesticides give me a headache," Tim was angry, but decided that discretion was the better part of valor. He reluctantly agreed to move the computer back into the house to keep the peace.

One day Julie returned from the gym to find that her new engagement ring from Skiadopoulos had disappeared, along with her CD player. Convinced that Katie had taken them she confronted her little daughter, who merely smiled, replying, "The ghost took the ring," and ran off.

Julie took care of all the preparations to bring Skiadopoulos to New Jersey. She booked and paid for his plane tickets on Northwest Airlines (getting a round-trip ticket as the one-way fare she had wanted was almost double), made an appointment for him to get a hair transplant, and bought him a smart new set of clothes, so he wouldn't show her up in front of her friends. She even planted new flowers in her front garden so his very first glimpse of her home would be perfect.

After she finished gardening, Julie went up to the office to telephone Skiadopoulos. Uncharacteristically, he told her he was busy and would call her back soon.

When he failed to do so she was crushed, her imagination running rampant.

Julie had never forgotten about his previous affair with the Dutch crew member, and she had become uneasy about a recent fax he had sent, boasting of going to the ship's disco with a friend.

"I could tell that there was something different in your voice from the moment you said the first hello," she wrote that night, close to tears.

I think it sounded to me like a lack of passion in your voice. Now I know that it was one of duty because you knew that I was waiting for your call. This scares me.

Yes, I've been waiting for your call *all* afternoon. In fact, I've been waiting since 2:00 p.m. I thought you might call early because sometimes you do. I'm sorry if you think I should remember the schedule. Because I don't remember, does that matter?

Also, I have to admit that I was happy to hear when you said that you had no desire to go [to the disco]. So, I was shocked to hear that you went out, especially for so long that you only slept for two hours. How *should* I react? Are you *deliberately* trying to make me jealous? Is the friend that invited you a girl? You didn't say. I feel like you put a knife in my heart!

Nothing is more important to me than you are. You always tell me that I'm number one but then you tell me that you have to hang up after talking only five minutes. I don't understand. Now I think that there is something else you're not telling me. Why did it take two questions for you to tell me?

Is there something else? Should I ask again?

If there's something to tell me, *please* tell me at once so I don't misunderstand. I trust you but if you seem to be avoiding something, it makes me wonder why you don't want to tell me?

"I try and do everything to make you smile. I like to. Because I love you so much. Why did you say that my love is going down? Don't you know that it hurts me *every* time you say that? Probably not, because I never told you. Well, now you know. I hate it when you say that. Please don't say it again. I DON'T FEEL HAPPY NOW.

Within hours George had reassured her that there was nothing to worry about and that it was all in her mind. Indeed, he even pledged to go straight up to the bridge and broadcast "I love Julaki," through the Galaxy's public address system.

On Saturday, August 22, Mary Jones drove to New Jersey to visit Julie. It was the first time the school friends had seen each other in months, and Mary had already made it clear that she wanted nothing to do with Skiadopoulos when he came.

As soon as she arrived, she asked Julie about her future plans. Breathlessly, Julie told her that she had *never* experienced a love like this before, saying she hoped Mary would one day find true love.

"She was delusional," remembered Mary. "And she was very upset."

When Jones asked her what she would do in Greece, Julie answered that she was setting Skiadopoulos up in business with his own taxi service, out of the settlement money she expected from Tim.

"I told her it sounded like a soap opera and she just laughed," said Mary. "I told her she was living recklessly and she later held that comment against me."

When she left to drive home, Mary felt sad, hardly recognizing her oldest friend from the happy-go-lucky girl she had once known. It would be the last time she would ever see Julie.

CHAPTER THIRTEEN

COMING TO NEW JERSEY

On Friday, August 28, George Skiadopoulos arrived at Newark Airport at 9:26 p.m. aboard Northwest Airline's Flight 766 from Vancouver via Minneapolis. Julie was at the gate to meet him and rushed into his arms for an emotional reunion. As she drove him back to Mansfield Township, he proudly told her how he had slipped through American immigration on a visitor's visa, claiming to be a trainee fireman attending a seminar in New York.

Julie had ensured they would be alone for the weekend, arranging for Katie to stay at her grandmother's in Philadelphia. So Julie and Skiadopoulos spent most of the next couple of days making love and discussing their future in Greece.

On Sunday night, Julie called her mother and asked her to come over with Katie. It was agreed that Julia Scully would live in the basement with her granddaughter for the duration of Skiadopoulos's stay in New Jersey.

Julia Scully was full of trepidation when she arrived at the house on Tuesday morning. She strongly disapproved of Julie, who was still officially married to Tim, bringing her lover to his house. But there was little she could do to stop it.

When she let herself in through the front door, Julie and George were still in bed. Eventually Julie appeared, asking how long she and Katie had been there. Then she went upstairs and brought George Skiadopoulos down to meet her mother and daughter.

"I had thought at least he must be some kind of handsome Greek god," said Julia. "But when I first saw him I thought he was a short, ugly-looking freak. He was going bald and he gave me the chills."

Julia was speechless as George put his arm around Julie and began saying how much he loved her. When she politely offered him her hand, Skiadopoulos pulled Julie even closer into his arms as he shook it.

"And I thought to myself, 'I don't like this guy,'" remembered Julia. "He's after her money."

Over the next few days Skiadopoulos went out of his way to impress Julia, continually telling her how much he loved her daughter. Katie took an immediate dislike to the new man in her mother's life, keeping out of his way as much as possible.

Julie had not bothered to inform Tim that Skiadopoulos was coming, so she tried to stop him from coming to the house. But eventually Katie told her father that George had moved in. Tim was livid.

"And that's when I confronted Julie," said Tim. "I said, 'I really don't like the fact that he's here with you.

If you're carrying on another romance, that's entirely up to you. But not when it involves my daughter.' "

Julie tried to placate Tim and lied, saying that George was only staying for a few days and would then leave. After months of wrangling, the estranged couple were close to reaching a settlement and neither of them wanted a setback. They both desperately wanted to get it over with, so they could move on with their lives.

"We weren't that far apart," said Tim of the couple's negotiations. "We were probably within a hundred grand of each other."

It was not long before George Skiadopoulos was acting like the man of the house, and Julie seemed to love his taking control. She telephoned all her friends and put George on the line. He would then tell them how much he loved Julie and how lucky he was to have found her.

But he was careful to keep Julie as far away as possible from her remaining friends, whom he viewed as a threat.

"George called me on the car phone," recounted Sue White. "I remember he said, 'Maybe we'll have you over for dinner next week.' It was very obvious that he did not want me around."

When Sue and her five-year-old son Robbie finally came to dinner, George was at the door to greet them. Taking her to one side, he asked how long she was going to stay. Taken aback, Sue replied that she would try and eat her dinner as fast as possible.

It was a strained evening and Sue felt uncomfortable around Skiadopoulos, who refused to let her be alone with Julie.

"Julie wanted to talk to me and he would not leave us for one second," she said. "I don't know what she saw in him. He wasn't attractive at all and I thought,

'Well, maybe he has a good personality.' "

Sue also noticed how George pretended that his English was limited, but always seemed to pick up on her jokes.

"Julie would feel that she would have to translate what I was saying," said Sue. "Yet he knew English. I guess that was a way of making her feel needed."

Sue and Robbie White left the house as soon as possible. On the drive home the little boy remarked how indifferent Skiadopoulos seemed toward Katie, never once speaking to her the entire time they were there.

During her marriage to Tim, Julie had amassed an expensive wardrobe, having spent thousands of dollars on fashionable dresses and jewelry. Several times a week she went to the beauty parlor to have her nails done and had her own masseuse, who had become a personal friend.

So when George arrived in New Jersey she immediately gave him a makeover, so she wouldn't have to feel ashamed. She took him out shopping to a mall, fitting him out in smart new clothes. Then they proceeded to her jewelers, where she ordered a $600 gold bracelet for him with her pet name "JULAKA" engraved on it.

But when she called Mary Jones, asking if she would fill George's cavity-ridden teeth, the dental surgeon refused. Later Mary would say how "disgusting" it was that he had such poor personal hygiene at such a young age.

"I thought he had zero character," said Jones. "It was in poor taste for him to have slept in the bedroom of the house that Tim owned with Tim's wife."

A few weeks earlier Julie had spotted a magazine advertisement for a new hair-restoring treatment, which claimed great successes with rock stars and actors. She had made an appointment for Skiadopoulos to have the $1,600 "Permanent European Baldness Treatment" at her expense in Voorhees, New Jersey. The vain sailor was only too happy to undergo the painful operation, which inserted hairs into the scalp to thicken hairlines and "produce a natural, individual growing effect."

On their return to the house, Julie warned her mother not to stare at George or he'd become self-conscious about his new look.

"It really didn't bother me because he didn't interest me one way or the other," said Julia Scully. "But I was upset that he had all these new clothes on and Julie was paying for everything."

Julia and Skiadopoulos disliked each other right from the beginning and the forceful woman had no qualms telling him exactly what she thought of him. She considered him rude and arrogant, hating the fact that the Greek was sleeping in Tim's bed while Katie was in the house. Since his arrival Julie had had little time for Katie, leaving Julia to care for her granddaughter.

Most days George would stay in bed until lunch time and then go to the gym with Julie. After that he'd come home to change for a night out or he'd spend the evening in the Jacuzzi. The sailor did not appear to have any money so Julie paid for everything on her credit cards.

At first there was an uneasy truce between Julia and Skiadopoulos, but it wasn't long before tempers flared.

"I thought he behaved like a love-struck sixteen-year-old," said Julia. "It was pathetic. They would make big paper signs, saying, 'Julie and George Forever,' and hang them in her room. It was so childish.

"I told George, 'You're here and you're not even married and living in another man's house. You're not a man!' "

Most of Julie's friends stayed away from the house when George was there. Sue White and her sisters were the only ones to meet him face-to-face. Everybody suspected that Skiadopoulos was systematically turning Julie against them and felt uncomfortable even talking to her on the phone, as he was always hovering in the background, listening.

On several occasions Cheryl Chuplis made plans to meet Julie and Skiadopoulos, but these were always canceled at the last minute by Julie, with some lame excuse.

"It got to the point where I was a little disgusted," said Cheryl. "I really think he influenced Julie, because she was not like that at all."

Once Cheryl called the house and George picked up the phone. Trying to be polite, she asked him how he was enjoying New Jersey and he said he liked it. But when she asked about Katie, he replied, "Oh, she's very spoiled."

On one occasion, Skiadopoulos said he would teach Katie how to play piano after boasting to Julia that he knew all about children and had brought up his brother and sister. But the piano lesson never materialized and when Julia asked her daughter if Skiadopoulos had a piano of his own in Greece, she said no.

Julie and Skiadopoulos saw the one big obstacle to their future happiness as his military service. Under Greek law every young man has to serve up to two years in the army and Skiadopoulos knew he would be called up in a few months. He and Julie became increasingly obsessed with finding ways he could dodge serving his country. Both were concerned that their relationship wouldn't survive so many months apart.

"Oh boy, was that a big thing," remembered Julia. "He was calling people all the time for help."

Having discarded the idea of Skiadopoulos remaining in the United States illegally, they explored the possibility of him registering at the University of Athens, so he could apply for a visa to study in America.

Julie also called her friend Tony Capella, asking him to use his highly placed political connections to help Skiadopoulos. Tony refused point-blank, saying that he wanted nothing to do with it.

It was a very difficult time for Tim Nist, knowing that George was in his home and having to go there several times a week to pick up Katie for her visits. With the divorce settlement proceedings nearing completion, he did not want to antagonize Julie, whose behavior was becoming more and more unpredictable.

"I felt taken advantage of," said Nist. "Everything was always, 'Send the bill to Tim.' "

Skiadopoulos was once again filling Julie's head with paranoid conspiracy theories, involving her friends and Tim. One afternoon he told her he suspected that Tim had bugged the house to eavesdrop on their conversations. So they decided to check.

Some years earlier, Tim had installed an elaborate stereo system in the basement with speaker wires running through a partition in the suspended ceiling. Skiadopoulos methodically ripped up all the ceiling tiles and pulled out the wires in a futile search for electronic bugs.

"What kind of paranoia is that?" asked Tim, who would later have to rewire the ceiling himself.

On the Saturday after Labor Day, Tony Capella held his annual summer party at his beach house on the Jersey Shore. Although he had made it clear to Julie several times that he didn't want her coming with Skiadopoulos, they both turned up anyway.

"She knew me well enough to know that if I had a bunch of people at my house I wouldn't cause a scene and throw them out," said Capella. "But I told her I wasn't happy that she'd brought him."

Throughout the party Skiadopoulos looked edgy and uncomfortable as Julie started drinking and introduced him to everyone as her new fiancé.

"He wouldn't talk to me," said Capella. "He was kind of rude and stand-offish. I was struck by the fact that he wasn't even handsome. You couldn't look at him and say, 'Oh, that's what she sees in him.' In fact, I couldn't figure out what she saw in him but he seemed to take some control over her."

A few days later Julie asked Sue White to come with her to buy a wedding dress, which she planned to take to Greece. In the bridal store while Katie and Robbie ran around and caused quite a stir, Julie tried on a selection of plain white dresses. She had put her hair up and she wanted a veil, as George had said that all Greek brides wear them for modesty.

"She was telling everyone how she was getting married in Greece and how it was different over there," said Sue.

Julie finally decided on a seven-hundred-dollar white dress with a train, but became upset when the alterations required almost doubled the price.

"Compared to the wedding dress she had married Tim in, this was a major step down," said Sue. "But then, she looked pretty in anything."

That night Julie and George were invited to a small get-together at Sue's house with the triplets and a few close friends. Once again Skiadopoulos was out of place and there was an uneasy silence when Julie introduced him as the new man in her life.

"Just from the way he shook [my friends'] hands you could tell he was trying to show his strength," said Sue. "It wasn't a nice, 'How do you do.' " He was trying to be macho."

During the evening Skiadopoulos appeared glued to Julie, even going as far as following her upstairs to the bathroom, and waiting outside for her to finish. After Julie and George left early, everyone agreed that they didn't like the Greek and foresaw problems ahead.

"Everyone said she was going to be sorry," said Sue. "Somebody even said that he would probably beat her, as that's the way the Greeks treat their women."

On September 21, Tim Nist had finally had enough of Julie's lack of work and fired her from Stirling Lawns. Although she was still collecting her weekly paycheck, she had not bothered to do anything since Skiadopoulos had arrived, and was charging their living expenses to the company.

After consulting his lawyer, who said he would probably save money by firing his estranged wife, Tim sent her a pink slip, asking her to turn over all the company records.

"She got pissed off and annoyed but there was nothing she could do about it," said Tim. "As chief executive I had to protect the company's interests and she was doing nothing."

A few days later Julie's attorney called, saying that the final divorce papers were ready for her to sign. The couple had finally reached a settlement with Tim agreeing to pay Julie $600,000 over the next few months.

But despite gaining her freedom, Julie seemed genuinely upset when she called Sue White to tell her the news.

"George must have been out at the store when she

called," said Sue. "I know that she didn't want him to be there when she signed."

Sue advised her friend to wait a few days, saying that there was no rush to sign the divorce papers, which would officially terminate her marriage to Tim. But two hours later Julie called back to say she had signed, explaining that George had come back and taken her out for a couple of drinks to relax her first.

"He didn't drink," said Sue. "He talked to her and all of a sudden she's ready to go and sign the papers. That was not good."

On the way home from the attorney, Julie arrived alone at Sue White's house in a highly distressed condition. She was upset that the divorce was now final and seemed uncertain about her relationship with Skiadopoulos, now that they had spent some time together on her home turf.

"She talked about George and how she now saw him differently," said Sue, "and that her feelings for him were decreasing. She was beginning to have doubts."

Then Julie wanted to go out to a bar for a few drinks and called Skiadopoulos to ask him to join them. As soon as they all arrived, Julie started knocking back a succession of double Absolut vodkas on the rocks, while they played pool in the back bar. At first she seemed upset but as the alcohol took effect, she seemed to calm down.

At one point she went off to the restroom leaving Sue alone with Skiadopoulos.

"He began talking to me," said Sue. "He was trying to convince me what a great thing he had with Julie and I was questioning it. Then he started saying the exact same words she had said to me earlier about him. It was like a parody. I felt she had been brainwashed and had lost her personality."

During his stay in America, Julie had planned a trip to Orlando so George could meet her brother's family and visit Disney World. But at the last minute they canceled and telephoned John Scully to tell him.

"George came on the phone," said John. "It was a very general conversation and I just asked him how things were going."

Then in his thick accent Skiadopoulos declared his great love for John's sister, saying that he put her on a pedestal.

"He said he worshipped her and it seemed like he loved her a lot," said John. "That was fine with me."

In late September, Julie officially introduced Skiadopoulos to the rest of the Scullys at their annual family reunion at Dennisville Lake, New Jersey, where she had gone camping as a little girl. A week earlier she had called her father, breaking the news that she had divorced Tim and was bringing her new fiancé to the reunion.

Skiadopoulos was on his best behavior as he was introduced to the Scully family and then sat down with them for a picnic lunch.

"I thought they were like a couple of young kids in love," remembered Julie's father. "She was in love with him so there wasn't anything I can say."

Visibly uncomfortable in another social situation, George trailed behind Julie the entire day, making a point of holding her hand at every opportunity.

"Julie told me that she thinks she is going to marry him," said John Senior. "That he worships the ground she walks on and all that stuff. That's when I told her about the Greeks, because they don't want the women to have opinions and what they say, goes. And my daughter Julie's a very headstrong young lady. She does what *she* wants to do."

During lunch, Julie's father asked his future son-in-law about his prospects, saying that his own son was an electronics engineer in the U.S. Navy.

"He began to boast, telling me that he worked on the second-largest ship in the world. So I figured that the guy might be able to get himself a decent-paying job."

On October 7th, Skiadopoulos finally dropped his guard, unable to suppress his volatile temper any longer. When Julie got into an argument with her mother over recording a children's video for Katie, Skiadopoulos lashed out, grabbing the middle-aged woman around the neck and trying to strangle her.

"He was yelling and pounding on the wall," remembered Julia. "He had a terrible temper."

Shaken by George's violent outburst, Julie tried pulling him off her mother, saying that he'd get in trouble, while Julia screamed that he was going to jail. Finally, Skiadopoulos relaxed his grip on Julia's neck, telling her *never* to speak to his fiancée like that again. Julia told him it was none of his business and ran out of the room.

When Tim returned to his apartment that afternoon he found a message from Julia, asking him to call her urgently. Tim telephoned and Julia said she *must* see him right away about something important.

When Tim arrived at Mansfield Road, a visibly distressed Julia came outside barefoot to meet him. She told him that Skiadopoulos had tried to strangle her and showed him the large bruises on her neck. Then Julie came rushing out to try and calm things down. But Tim said he was going straight to the police.

An hour later at Mansfield Township Police Station, Julia Scully swore out a complaint against Skiadopoulos for simple assault. Then Tim accompanied two police officers back to the house, where George Skiadopoulos was arrested and driven to the police station. After taking his mug shot he was processed, fingerprinted and thrown in a cell.

In desperation Julie called Tony Capella and asked him to post bail. She was in tears as she explained how her mother was accusing Skiadopoulos of trying to strangle her.

"I said, 'I'm not going to bail him out,' " said Capella. " 'I don't like him to begin with. This is more evidence that this is the wrong thing for you to do.' Then she got mad at me and hung up."

Initially the police had wanted to free Skiadopoulos on bail, but Tim was determined that he not return to the house while Katie was there. So he made a deal with the prosecutor to prevent George from ever coming back: in exchange for Julia withdrawing her complaint, the police agreed to put Skiadopoulos on a plane back to Greece. Reluctantly, Julia agreed to the arrangement and rescinded her complaint.

"Julie was mad at me," said Tim. "She said, 'Well, thanks for contributing to my happiness.' "

Under the agreement Skiadopoulos could not return to the house before he left the country. So once again Julie called Tony Capella for help, asking if they could stay at his beach house until he could get a flight.

"I said that wasn't going to happen," recalled Tony. "I said, 'You and Katie will always have a bed in my house but not him.' Then she goes, 'Fuck you!' and slammed down the phone again."

A few days later Skiadopoulos left for Greece. Even

though Julie had now witnessed his uncontrollable temper, she immediately booked herself a plane ticket so she could join him there the following week, telling her friends that *she* was to blame for the attack.

"Julie swore to me that she had grabbed her mother," said Tracey Buehler, "and she said the reason why was because Julia called her a bad mother and said she was taking Katie away."

Julie also told Sue White that she had attacked her mother and scratched her neck, claiming George had sprung to Julia's rescue and pulled her off.

"She lied to the lot of us," said Sue. "Because she knew that if I found out the truth, that would have been it."

A few days after Skiadopoulos's dramatic departure, Julie sat down and put her innermost thoughts in her private notebook. Her words, which were underlined, reveal the torturous struggle now going on in her head:

I will not loathe myself, I will not loathe myself. Self-pity will not control my life. Small steps everyday [sic] will convert self-loathing into self-loving!!

Look at yourself naked. Blessed am I to live in such a beautiful temple. Blessed am I to love in such a beautiful temple.

CHAPTER FOURTEEN

THE LEAVING

Soon after George Skiadopoulos flew back to Greece, Tim Nist heard through friends that Julie was planning to take their daughter to live there. He was furious. It was one thing for her to go across the world to marry Skiadopoulos, but quite another matter when it involved his three-year-old child. So he immediately called Julie to discuss Katie's future.

"I said, 'You can't just take Katie,'" Tim recalled. "'Because if you do I'll come and get her, and you'll never see her again.'"

When Julie refused to back down, Tim threatened to go to court and fight her for his daughter's custody.

"I told Julie she would lose that case. I have the job, I have the house, I have the family, I have the relatives—they're all here. I said, 'You're just not going to take my kid and run around Europe with $600,000.'"

For once Julie would not get her own way. Tim had the full support of her mother and her friends, who all agreed that taking a three-year-old child to Greece would cause her irreparable harm. And Julie also remembered being dragged through the Philadelphia Family Court by her own parents as a young girl.

"I told Julie, 'This country is not like America,' " said her mother. 'Katie doesn't belong there. She doesn't speak the language. And what if she got ill over there?' I tried to talk her out of it."

Realizing that no American court would ever grant her custody to take Katie abroad, Julie abandoned the idea and determined to go to Greece alone.

"And that's what really threw her apart," said Cheryl Chuplis. "She didn't know what to do because she said to me, 'I have to go because I've never felt like this before in my life and if I don't [go] we're going to lose that love we have. I *need* to get married to him.' "

On October 20, the day after her divorce became final, Julie flew to Athens and into the arms of George Skiadopoulos. It was her first time in Europe and she felt a great sense of exhilaration now that her great adventure was finally starting.

The plan was for her and George to stay in Athens one week and then go to Kavala to meet his family. Then she would return to the United States to arrange to ship over her possessions, before moving permanently at the beginning of December.

During the one-hour drive into Athens, Julie felt she had made the right decision, as she told George about her $600,000 settlement, saying she was now a wealthy woman in her own right. He was delighted as they discussed his scheme to start a taxi business in Kavala.

It was a clear, sunny day and as Skiadopoulos drove through the sprawling Athens suburbs, Julie was spellbound by the Mediterranean-style, low-rise Greek architecture, which looked like nothing she had ever seen before. She soon acclimatized to the frenetic pace of Athens and always had a Greek phrase book in hand, to practice the few phrases George had taught her.

Although his father Pavlos lived in Athens, and Skiadopoulos had not seen him in more than a year, they stayed with his aunt, who lived just outside the city. Amazingly, George never contacted him once while they were in the city, and a worried Pavlos called Sue White several times, inquiring about his son's whereabouts.

On their first night in Athens, Skiadopoulos took Julie to dinner in Plaka. They sat at one of the many traditional Greek restaurants that litter the sidewalk in the shadow of the Acropolis. While they ate their meal and sipped wine, a procession of scrawny stray cats came up to the table, and Julie fed all of them.

Afterwards they went to visit the magnificent ancient ruins of the Acropolis and Julie was mesmerized by the sense of history. Naturally inquisitive, she asked some of the souvenir stall–holders questions about it and was disappointed to discover that they knew little more than what was in her guidebook.

While in Athens they became embroiled in Greek bureaucracy, as Julie submitted applications to get herself an official I.D. card and the necessary paperwork required for marriage. Every night they went out into downtown Athens, drinking and dancing into the small hours, then Skiadopoulos would drive her back to his aunt's apartment.

On October 25, they made the forty-five-minute flight to George's birthplace of Kavala, four hundred miles north of Athens near the Bulgarian border. It was early morning when Julie caught her first glimpse of her new home, as Kavala suddenly emerged through the thick, white clouds below. She gripped George's hand for reassurance as the small Olympic Airways plane set its wheels down on the runway.

The tiny airport was bathed in bright sunshine as they walked from the plane to the terminal, to pick up their hired car for the twenty-minute drive into town. Skiadopoulos took the wheel and careened out of the airport parking lot and onto a narrow twisting road, bordered by vine trees.

For months Julie had dreamed of this moment and the dramatic countryside didn't let her down. There was an ethereal quality in the diffused early morning light, which seeped through a translucent white haze onto the lonely flatlands below.

But where the farmlands she was used to in Mansfield Township were lush and green, the ones now stretching away from the road were barren and littered with stony hills.

Entering Kavala, dirty industrial smoke spewed high into the sky from a tobacco factory as they drove under Suleiman the Magnificent's Kamares Aqueduct. On the left were the stark ruins of a sixteenth century Byzantine castle set atop a large hill, with a motley jumble of white houses cascading down to the sea.

Skiadopoulos had made reservations for them to stay at the 1950s-style Galaxy Hotel on Erithrou Stavrou, the main drag by the harbor. The irony of the hotel sharing its name with the ship where they had met was not lost on Julie, who saw it as a good omen.

Although the summer tourist season was almost over, there were still plenty of bars and night clubs open for business. But unlike Athens few people spoke English, as hardly any foreign tourists ever made it this far north, preferring the more scenic Greek islands.

That night George's mother held a party at her house so Julie could officially meet the family. Beforehand, George had warned her not to mention that she had been married and had a child, as his staunchly Greek Orthodox family would disapprove and think her immoral.

Julie felt that her first meeting with his mother, grandmother and various aunts and uncles was successful. She got on especially well with his younger sister Maria and her feeble attempts to use her few Greek phrases brought howls of good-natured laughter.

"Julie was a lovely girl," said Skiadopoulos's godmother, Elini. "He loved her so much."

But his family was puzzled as to why a beautiful, wealthy American woman would want to move to a poor, shabby town like Kavala. When they asked her about it, Julie proudly pointed to her engagement ring, saying it was because of love. Although George's mother had some reservations about the six-year age difference, she hugged and kissed Julie and gave the couple her blessing.

The next day they went to a real estate agent and began searching for a house to live in after their wedding. By Kavala standards Julie was a rich American woman and Skiadopoulos wanted to move her into the best area in town.

He also caught up with old friends he hadn't seen for years, asking their advice on how to start a taxi business, as he proudly introduced Julie as his fiancée. His old school friend Alexis Makezedis, who now ran his own photography business, met Julie when George brought her into his shop to have their film of the Acropolis developed.

"George told me they were in love and he was crazy about her," said Makezedis. "but Julie didn't say very much and seemed cooler about displaying emotions than he did. They always wanted to go out clubbing but I was always too busy because of my business."

Every night George and Julie would party into the early morning, doing the round of Kavala's strip of night clubs and discotheques. Although George hardly drank, Julie would down a slew of exotic cocktails through the evening, often returning to the hotel drunk.

Sue White believes that on at least one occasion Skia-dopoulos lost his temper and beat Julie during that trip: When she returned she had "Frankenstein stitches" on her arm. When questioned about it, Julie claimed she had pushed her hand through a glass door."

But whatever happened, when Julie flew back to America on November 8, she was determined to return to Kavala within a month and marry George Skiadopou-los.

Back at Mansfield Road, Julie bought a $740 one-way ticket on Tower Air to Athens and began packing her things to be shipped over. Tim paid the first $120,000 installment of the settlement and under the terms of equitable distribution, she would continue to receive $5,000 a month until the $600,000 was paid off.

Under their agreement, Tim was allowed to move back into the house thirty days after the first payment of the settlement. So he was furious when Julie told him to send the first payment when she came back from Greece, giving herself an extra two weeks in the house.

"I said, 'You bitch . . . I wanted to give it to you before you left,' " said Tim. "She said that was not in the contract."

Sue White was again a constant visitor to the house and pleaded with Julie to leave some of her settlement money in a safety deposit box in America, in case things didn't work out.

"I said, 'Julie, this is the only thing I ask,' " remembered Sue. "Don't tell anyone about it and that way you'll have something to fall back on so you won't be stuck if anything goes wrong."

In the middle of their conversation Skiadopoulos telephoned from Greece and Julie naively mentioned putting some of her money in a safety deposit. George was furious, accusing her of thinking that he was only with her for her money. When he started trying to make her feel guilty, Julie slammed the phone down on him. But when he failed to call back she was devastated.

"I said, 'Don't worry about it,' " said Sue. 'He's playing games and is probably waiting by the phone for you to call.' "

As Sue White was still close to Tim Nist, it hurt her to witness the little things Julie now did to hurt him. After ordering the biggest shipping container available, she proceeded to pack it with everything she could. Although they still had nowhere to live in Kavala, Julie insisted on taking heavy marble garden furniture and some of Katie's clothes, even though the little girl was remaining behind.

"I mean, it was so petty and there was no room for it over there," said Sue. "I would say, 'Julie, what are you gaining by taking one of Tim's pictures just to get back at him?' "

Sue White spent most of her time with Julie and now barely recognized her friend. Where once Julie had been fun to be with and would do anything for a laugh, she had become distant and introspective. Sue began to suspect that she was having second thoughts about going to Greece.

"I thought she was mad at me for giving her advice and telling her not to go," said Sue. "I have a son and I just could not see [her] leaving Katie behind. But I think it was something else. Now she had come so far she couldn't admit to her friends that she had been wrong."

In her secret notebook Julie carefully listed her reservations about Skiadopoulos after her two weeks in Greece, wondering whether he was mature enough to take care of her.

> *This is what I wanted. I need to leave this place. I want to experience a new culture. I'm in love with George. He's the sweetest, most thoughtful person I have ever met. The thing that bothers me is his age. He is six years younger than me. I worry that he has not had a lot of life experience to help me to maintain my happiness in Kavala.*

> *I really wonder what he knows about maintaining a house, shopping, working (not on board etc.) I wish that he was at least my age. There is nothing that we can do to change this.*

On November 21, Julie called her brother in what would be their last-ever conversation. John Scully found her depressed about leaving Katie, as if she wanted to leave as soon as possible to get it over with.

"She didn't seem very enthusiastic about going to Greece," said John, who was leaving for a long naval assignment aboard a submarine the following day. "She knew the day was coming when she would separate from her friends and family.

"She knew it would mean a lot of pain leaving Katie

and she just wanted to get on with her new life. I told her that I loved her and I supported her in whatever she did."

The following day Julie organized a party at Mansfield Road, which was now almost bare of furniture, to celebrate Katie's third birthday. It was the Sunday before Thanksgiving—which was Katie's actual birthday—and many of Julie's friends attended to wish her well before she left for Greece.

Julie seemed in unusually good spirits as she welcomed them and helped Katie unwrap her presents. But there was an undercurrent of tension as her guests wondered how she could possibly abandon her beautiful little daughter.

It was the first time Katie's godfather, Tony Capella, had spoken to Julie since she'd slammed down the phone on him after the attack on Julia.

"We had a very cold 'hello,'" remembers Capella. "She was sitting at the kitchen table and she wasn't herself."

Julie began talking about her trip to Greece and how she really loved it there. But she said there was one thing she had really missed in Kavala.

"And I remember thinking for that split second, 'Oh, let her redeem herself. Please let her just say she missed her daughter while she was in Greece. If she says that, I might be able to at least get back a little bit of respect.' And then she said the thing she missed most was not having anywhere to get her nails done!"

Tony felt "sick to his stomach" on hearing her say that and left the table to go down to the basement, where Tim and his sister were talking. After regaining his composure he went back upstairs to leave.

"I had a very bland good-bye with Julie and she gave me a high-five," he recalled. "She said, 'Well, are you going to come to Greece and see me?' And I said, 'I don't think so.' And that was the last time I ever saw Julie."

When Cheryl Chuplis saw Julie on December 4, two days before she was due to leave, she found her old modeling partner in low spirits and utterly stressed out. Over the past few weeks Cheryl had called Julie on numerous occasions, but she had always been too busy to see her because of the move. However this time Julie had called Cheryl for a favor, asking her to pick up her wedding dress and bring it over before they went out for dinner.

"I walked into the house and it looked so empty," said Cheryl. "Julie was just a mess and exhausted because she hadn't been sleeping."

At the restaurant Julie downed a succession of double Absoluts on the rocks before she finally seemed to relax and unwind. Then she began telling Cheryl about her latest plans in Greece.

"I asked her when she was going to get married," Cheryl said, "and she told me George's parents wanted them to have a Greek wedding. They were even thinking about having kids because that would shorten his military service.

"I thought she seemed unsure and, although you could tell she was trying to be strong and straightforward about it, she was confused. By this time he [George] was calling her every minute of the day."

Cheryl agreed to come and visit Julie in Greece the following March, but when she dropped her friend off at home she had an uneasy feeling about how things would pan out.

Sunday, December 6, was unseasonably warm with temperatures in Philadelphia hitting seventy degrees. That morning Tim Nist dropped Katie off with her grandmother, as Julie had to take care of some last-minute business in Trenton before she flew to Greece that night.

It was late afternoon when Julia brought the little girl back to Mansfield Road to find that Julie had already started drinking to calm her nerves. Soon afterwards Tim arrived at the house. He was moving back in as soon as Julie left to catch the night flight to Athens.

"I could tell Julie had a few drinks in her," remembers Tim. "She was pretty drunk."

Julie was very emotional and close to tears as she said good-bye to Katie and hugged and kissed her in the front room. Susan White was waiting outside with a truck to take Julie to the airport and, as the minutes ticked by, Tim hurried her up, saying she would miss her flight if she didn't leave soon.

"She was trying to find a way to say good-bye to Katie and she was very upset," said Tim. "I said, 'Hey, Julie, you've just got to go. It's not going to be any different ten minutes from now.'"

At last Julie composed herself and kissed Katie and her mother, who both waved farewell as Sue White pulled out from the driveway and headed out towards Kennedy Airport. There was little traffic at that time of night and they reached the Tower Air terminal with plenty of time to spare.

As Sue's truck was loaded up with things Julie had given her, she waited for Julie to go into the terminal and check in. After twenty minutes, when Julie failed to come out again, Sue drove around the terminal asking what had happened to the passengers.

She was told that Flight F32 had boarded earlier than planned and Julie was already in her seat, waiting to take off for Athens.

PART THREE

GREEK TRAGEDY

CHAPTER FIFTEEN

KAVALA BLUES

When Julie Scully flew into Kavala with George Skiadopoulos on Tuesday, December 8, she was shocked to find it shut down for the winter. It was cold and raining and most of the clubs and bars had now closed their doors until April. It was completely different from the sunny resort town Julie had seen two months earlier and not at all what she had been expecting.

After hiring a car at the airport they drove straight to the home of George's mother, where they were to stay until they could find their own apartment. There, waiting to welcome Julie, was George's entire family. Julie did her best to be friendly and sociable but only George spoke English and her Greek was limited to just a few words.

The following day they got up early and went straight to the National Bank of Greece, where Julie opened a joint account for herself and George, depositing a certified check for $80,000. She was also carrying $18,000 in cash.

Later, when her friends found out about the joint account they were amazed that she would have given Skiadopoulos control over her finances.

"This was not Julie," said Sue White. "She was always very stingy with her money and when I found out about the joint account I knew something was not right."

Right from the beginning Julie felt uneasy in Kavala, struggling to come to grips with her new life. Suddenly everything seemed foreign. She couldn't read the newspapers, understand the TV, or communicate with anyone except George. She felt like a stranger.

His family did their best to make her feel at home and tried to include her in conversations as much as possible. But the small northern Greek town had little to offer Julie in terms of the twenty-four-hour amenities and non-stop action she was used to in New Jersey. Before long Julie started feeling homesick for her old friends and her daughter Katie.

"The first week she didn't call at all," said Tim Nist, who had by then moved back into his house with Julie's mother and Katie. "I thought it was strange and wondered if she missed Katie. But then she started calling all the time to talk to Katie."

"She missed her daughter Katie more and more each day," Skiadopoulos would later relate. "Every time she would call, Julie would cry." In fact, nearly every day she would call first Katie, and then her friends, desperately needing to make a connection with home. But as always, Skiadopoulos was by her side, so she would say little of substance.

Skiadopoulos and Julie soon settled down into a routine. Most days they roamed around Kavala looking for apartments, and at night they would meet George's old friends for cocktails. The boastful Skiadopoulos loved trying and impress everyone with stories of his illustrious career on the Galaxy; Julie sat by his side drinking, unable to understand what was being said.

As Julie became more and more restless, she began finding fault with almost everything about Kavala. It was too remote, far closer to Bulgaria than the closest Greek city, Salonika, seventy-five miles to the southwest. She complained that Greek people were lazy because the town closed up for siesta three hours each afternoon. The food was full of grease, she said, and made her sick.

"Every day Julie would emphasize the differences between Greece and the United States," said Skiadopoulos. "This made me very concerned for our future."

One night they were in a night club drinking when the disk jockey took off the American disco music Julie had been dancing to, putting on traditional Greek songs instead. Julie was furious. She stormed up to the DJ and caused a big scene, demanding that he take off that trash and stick to American pop music.

"She was drunk," said Skiadopoulos's school friend Alexis Makezedis, who was in the club at the time. "George had to go to the owner and apologize on her behalf. He was very embarrassed."

Most nights they went out to their favorite bar at the Hotel Galaxy, where Julie would proceed to drink cocktail after cocktail as George sipped beer. She would then telephone her friends in New Jersey, pretending that everything was fine.

On December 17, there was a snowstorm and Julie retired to her bedroom at George's mother's house to write postcards to Cheryl Chuplis and Sue White.

"Hey Cher, This is where I live. What do you think?"

wrote Julie on the back of a card, showing a harbor view of the town. "I miss you and especially my little stinker Katie, but for the most part I'm happy. Talk to you soon, Love Julie."

In a card to Sue, Julie complained that the hired Hyundai she was now driving was a far cry from the Cadillac she had been used to. She also pointed out that the snow in Kavala was not as good as they got in New Jersey. But for some reason Julie never mailed the cards, packing them away in her suitcase.

Five days later, Simos Skiadopoulos discovered that Julie had been married and had a little daughter. She was horrified and started screaming at Julie in Greek. George rushed to her defense. In traditional Greek culture, the idea of a mother abandoning a child to live with a man is beneath contempt and Simos told Julie to leave her house immediately.

So George and Julie packed up their things and moved into the Egnatia Hotel, where they would spend Christmas.

The Egnatia was the best hotel in Kavala—but there was little competition. It was also the most expensive and, although Skiadopoulos managed to cut a deal with the owner for a discount, they could not afford to stay there indefinitely, as it was a drain on Julie's money.

Pressure was mounting on the couple, whose future now looked uncertain. Skiadopoulos had been ordered to report to an army barracks early next year to begin military service. Julie had agreed that they would marry before he went and then she would wait for him in Greece.

On Christmas Eve they went to a party with some of Skiadopoulos's friends and Julie got very drunk. At about midnight she decided that she wanted to wish Katie a merry Christmas. She found a phone and eventually tracked Tim down to his sister Jean's home, where it was five o'clock in the afternoon.

"I could tell she had been drinking," said Tim. "And she goes, 'I want to talk to Katie.' I said she was asleep on the couch and I didn't want to wake her. So I handed the phone to my sister because I couldn't understand what Julie was saying."

On Christmas Day, Julie was slightly more coherent when she called again and spoke to her daughter, saying that she was having a wonderful time in Kavala. It was the first Christmas since Katie had been born that they had been apart and Julie was devastated. The lonelier she became, the more she argued with George.

On December 28, Julie and George were in their hotel room when they got into a huge fight after Julie complained about how inferior Greece was to America.

Suddenly Skiadopoulos's eyes glazed over and he grabbed Julie around the neck and tried to strangle her. His uncle, who was also there, finally managed to pull him off her and calm him down.

Julie was badly shaken up by the sheer violence of his attack. She could no longer pretend that George wasn't violent and, for the first time, she realized that he was dangerous.

Later a private detective would discover that Julie had wanted to press charges against Skiadopoulos, but was dissuaded from doing so by his relatives, who explained that although George was emotional, he was harmless.

A few minutes later the owner of the hotel came up to their room and asked them to leave, saying that there had been complaints from other guests who had been kept awake by their loud arguing. Once again they packed their suitcases and moved this time into the Hotel Galaxy, where they had stayed during Julie's first trip to Kavala.

Later that night a tearful Julie called Sue White. She said she could not talk about what had been happening but that she felt sick to her stomach.

"And then George grabbed the phone," said Sue. "I think she was being abused and was trying to give me a hint so I could figure it out. But he was always there so she couldn't talk."

George was now becoming desperate, fearing that when he left for his military service he would lose all control over Julie. As they discussed his future, Skiadopoulos suggested they go to America so he could avoid the draft. Julie refused, saying he would be there illegally without a green card and that Tim would prevent her having access to Katie.

On New Year's Day Julie called Julia and asked to speak to Katie. But since Julie had left, Katie had become difficult and moody and refused to talk to her. "Katie was *so* cranky," remembers her grandmother. "Julie left her daughter and the kid missed her."

Although George and Julie were arguing more than ever at the Hotel Galaxy, they were still trapped in a mutual dependency. Every morning the chambermaids would come in to clean the room, and find love notes from George scrawled on the bathroom mirror in Julie's lipstick.

Finally the couple found an apartment in Pior, the most expensive area in Kavala, and put down a year's deposit. Julie began shopping for furniture for their new home, which they planned to move into in a couple of weeks.

On Sunday, January 3, 1999, Julie turned thirty-one

and Skiadopoulos threw a surprise birthday party for her at his grandmother's house. She walked in to find the family waiting for her and was delighted.

The Christmas decorations were still up in the front room and Julie was all smiles as she posed with George, showing off her engagement ring. His grandmother, Tiriaki Papadopoulou, had baked a small white birthday cake which had a single black candle in the middle. Everyone applauded as she blew out the candle and kissed George tenderly.

She then posed for pictures with Skiadopoulos, who was wearing his new hairpiece and glasses. In one macabre shot his arm is reaching out around Julie's neck.

Later, she left the party to go outside to a pay phone and call her friends in America.

"She sounded so happy," said Cheryl Chuplis. "She told me that they had found a place and would soon be moving in. I said I'd come over and visit in March."

Then Julie became sad as she told Cheryl how much she missed Katie, complaining that whenever she tried to speak to her daughter, Julia or Tim would always pull the phone away.

"She must have called ten times on her birthday," said Tim. "She did speak to Katie but she had been drinking. I think Julie was wrestling within herself about what to do. She was all over the map."

The next day Julie received word that her containers with her possessions had finally arrived in Athens and was ready for her to come get them. But instead of being happy that all her worldly possessions had arrived, her spirits sank lower than ever. Once she picked them up and brought them to Kavala, she knew that there was no going back.

*   *   *

On Wednesday, January 6, Julie called Tracey Allen in a state of panic. It was noon in America and Tracey was at her desk at Lawrenceville College, New Jersey.

"I kept asking her what was wrong because she sounded so upset," said Tracey. "Then all of a sudden she started crying really hard, like she was hyperventilating. She said she missed Katie so much that she could not sleep or eat. Her stomach hurt so badly she thought she had an ulcer."

Tracey told her to come home if she was so miserable. But Julie said she was afraid to face all her friends after everything that had happened. Tracey told her that she would fix everything. She then suggested that Julie marry George in Greece and then return to America while he served his military obligation.

"Then George got on the phone with me," said Tracey. "He said that Julie was upset all the time and was not eating or sleeping. I said, 'Well, just marry her and send her home.' He agreed it was a good idea and handed the phone back to Julie."

Thrilled that her friend was coming home again, Tracey suggested places she could live to be near her daughter and promised to help her with arrangements. At the end of the conversation Tracey repeated their favorite saying, 'Yo, Girl, I got your back!" and Julie began giggling.

After putting down the phone Tracey immediately called Julia to tell her that Julie was coming home. But instead of being overjoyed, Julia was against the idea.

"I said, 'Julie's going to call you soon,' " Tracey recounted, "can't you just forget the past and love her because she's your daughter?' And she said, 'No.' "

Four hours later Julie called her mother and Tim picked up. When she broached the subject of coming home again, Tim also thought it was a bad idea, that it would be disruptive for Katie.

"I said, 'Katie's just getting her feet back on the ground,' " Tim recalled. "I asked her to hold off for a little while. She said that was OK and put the phone down."

A few minutes later Julie called Tim again. This time she asked him if Katie could come and visit her in Kavala instead.

"I told Julie that was not a good idea," he said. "and although I couldn't stop her from coming back to Mansfield and seeing Katie, she could not move back into the house."

From there the conversation deteriorated as Julie became emotional, desperately trying to find a way to be reconciled with her daughter. When she pleaded with Tim to send Katie over to Greece, he told her firmly, "It's not going to happen."

Julie then became hysterical, accusing her ex-husband of not caring about Katie's happiness.

"I said, 'Care about my daughter! You're the one who left.' Then she hung up on me."

A few minutes later Tim was taking a shower when he heard the phone ring and didn't answer. Later he checked the answering machine but there was no message on it.

"That was the last time anyone talked to her," said Tim. "The *very* last time."

CHAPTER SIXTEEN

THE ROAD TO SALONIKA

On Friday, January 8, George Skiadopoulos went with Julie to Kavala's city hall to take out a marriage license. Later they would drive to Athens to pick up Julie's belongings. They also planned to marry there on January 23, in a civic ceremony.

Since her last telephone call to Tim, Julie had been inconsolable, feeling like a trapped animal with nowhere to run. She longed to return to the States and see Katie, but despaired that even her family had rejected her. And she knew Tim would *never* allow her three-year-old daughter to come to Greece.

The walls were also closing in on Skiadopoulos. There had been an uneasy silence between them over the last couple of days. The usually talkative Julie had retreated into her own world, which George found he could no longer enter. The passion in their relationship had gone. They had done nothing but argue since Julie had come to Kavala and he knew he had lost his control over her. Her love had been replaced by fear after he had attacked her. All his dreams of marrying Julie and living a life of affluence and ease were disintegrating before his eyes.

Taking out the license was a sham; they both secretly knew the marriage would never take place. George Skiadopoulos was now convinced that Julie planned to escape at the first opportunity. There was only one way to prevent her from leaving him.

As they were preparing to leave for Athens, George's mother telephoned with the news that his younger brother had been taken ill and was in the hospital. When George and Julie arrived at Kavala Hospital they both appeared very upset and emotional, and as George spoke to his mother and sick brother, Julie became angry, anxious to set out for the long drive to Athens.

By the time they left at five in the afternoon, Skiadopoulos had made up his mind. If he couldn't have her, no other man ever would.

It was a cold, damp evening as Skiadopoulos headed west out of Kavala in their rented white Fiat Punto along the Aegean coastal road towards Salonika. From there, he told Julie, they would go south to Athens and stay at his father's house.

By the time they passed Kalamitsa Beach it was getting dark. Skiadopoulos remembered a beautiful October day when they had gone sunbathing there, but that was when they were still madly in love. Now his beautiful fiancée was a stranger and all his promises of finding true happiness in Greece had evaporated.

There was little traffic on the winding two-lane coastal highway as they drove through Nea Iraklitsa and Nea Peramos. It was a road Skiadopoulos was well acquainted with, having driven it many times with his father when he was a young boy.

Julie tried to break the tension by making small talk about the new apartment that they were due to move into when they returned from Athens. But after a few terse sentences they plunged into another argument, rehashing the same old problems that they had discussed over and over.

Julie sat back and contemplated leaving Skiadopoulos in Athens. Maybe if she disappeared for a few days she could get herself together and decide what her next move should be.

About twenty-five minutes out of Kavala they passed the tiny fishing village of Eleochori, and the road became even more desolate, a dark trail to nowhere. There was nothing between here and Loutra Eleftheron, twenty miles away.

They fell into silence again as Skiadopoulos slowed down the car, his steely eyes searching the rows upon rows of vineyards stretching off into the distance. It was a lonely stretch of road that his father used to take him to as a boy. No one ever came up here in the winter, especially on a rainy night like this. It was the perfect place to carry out his dark enterprise.

He finally saw a suitable opening and turned into it, telling Julie that he had to relieve himself. She felt an icy shiver run down her neck as she saw the desolate swamp loom up ahead in the bright headlights of the Fiat.

Skiadopoulos stopped the car, turned off the engine and slowly turned towards Julie in the passenger seat, summoning up his courage. There was a strange look on his face that Julie had never seen before, and it scared her.

Then, without saying a word, Skiadopoulos suddenly grabbed her by the throat and gripped her as tightly as he could. Julie started screaming in terror and tried to defend herself, but there was no one to hear her for miles.

"I went into a haze," Skiadopoulos would later confess. "She started yelling, 'What are you trying to do? I became scared and without wanting to I grabbed her harder to stop her screaming."

For three interminable minutes Skiadopoulos crushed Julie's neck with almost superhuman strength. When she gave up struggling and her body relaxed, he knew she was dead. Then he finally let go and Julie's lifeless body sank down into the passenger seat.

Completely out of breath and hyperventilating, Skiadopoulos's mind raced in a thousand different directions as he sat riveted to his seat, his unseeing eyes staring blankly out the window. It was like a dream. He looked at Julie in stunned disbelief, realizing that he had killed the one person who had ever really loved him. He would later claim that he tried to revive her without success.

But then a coldly calculating animal cunning took over. Turning off the headlights and sitting back next to Julie's dead body, he deliberated his next move. All he knew was that he must dispose of her body so he could stay free.

"From that moment on I couldn't think logically," he would later claim.

It could have been minutes or even hours before Skiadopoulos got out of the Fiat to clear his head. It was raining but he hardly noticed, pacing up and down the muddy dirt track, which seemed as forbidding as the depths of hell.

Just as their crazy passion had once expressed itself in cliché-ridden letters, Skiadopoulos now resolved to romanticize Julie's murder as the final chapter of their strange love story.

"As we had met at sea I first thought of tossing her body into the Aegean," he would explain.

He would later claim that he initially planned to burn his lover's body and scatter her ashes into the sea; then he would commit suicide.

Walking over to the passenger door, Skiadopoulos picked up Julie's body and placed it in the trunk of the car. Then he returned to the driver's seat, turned on the headlights and drove off the dirt track, turning right, back onto the national road toward Kavala.

Retracing the route he had driven with Julie, he stopped at a gas station in Nea Peramos to buy gasoline to burn her body. As he didn't have a jerry can he asked for directions to another station, where he bought a four-liter container, which he filled up with gas.

He then drove back to the national road and turned left toward Loutra Eleftheron, trying to find a secluded place to burn Julie's body. He drove past the dirt road where he had murdered her and slowed down looking for a suitable spot. He finally turned right onto another dirt track, just past the one-hundred-and-thirty-second kilometer sign on the road, and continued for fifty meters into a swamp.

"I saw that there were two small lakes next to each other, and stopped," Skiadopoulos would recall. "I took Julie's corpse out of the trunk and placed it by the side of the second lake. Then I doused her in gasoline and set her on fire."

It was still drizzling and damp outside and although Julie's clothes caught fire, her body would not. Frustrated, Skiadopoulos poured the entire container of gasoline over her, but his dead fiancée stubbornly refused to burn.

He then contemplated throwing her body into the muddy lake and started moving the body away from the Fiat to hide it. But he changed his mind and put it in a black garbage bag, throwing it back in the trunk of the car, and set off again toward Kavala.

Thirty minutes later, at around midnight, Skiadopoulos arrived at his grandmother's apartment and breathed a sigh of relief when he found that she was out. He let himself in and found, in a bedroom, a large black suitcase that he thought would hold Julie's body.

Returning to the Fiat with the suitcase, Skiadopoulos set off again for the half-hour journey to the two lakes, where he had decided to dispose of her. In the hours since the murder, he had ceased thinking of Julie as a real person. In his warped mind she had betrayed his love; now she would stay with him forever as they had both once sworn to do.

Back at the lakes he took her body out of the car and attempted to put it into the suitcase. Rigor mortis hadn't set in yet and her five-foot, seven-inch body was still pliable. But however hard he tried, he could not get Julie's entire body to fit the plastic case; her head kept protruding.

"Then I remembered there was a hacksaw in my grandmother's house," Skiadopoulos later told police. "I decided to get it so I could cut off her head."

Heading back to Kavala for the second time, Skiadopoulos returned to his grandmother's house, parking the car outside with Julie's body in the trunk. He went up to the attic and found the hacksaw and went back to the car, praying that he wouldn't see anyone he knew on the street.

It was about 2:30 a.m. when he once again drove the thirty-five miles to the lakes. After everything he had been through that night he was surprised at how calm and peaceful he now felt. At the one-hundred-and-thirty-second kilometer road sign he turned off yet again toward the two lakes and parked.

Taking Julie's body out of the trunk, he carried it to the side of the lake, placing it on a garbage bag. Then he went back to the Fiat for the iron hacksaw and began sawing off her head at the base of the neck. It surprised him at how hard it was to saw through bone and he was soon exhausted and covered in her blood.

When he finished his gruesome work he picked up Julie's head by her long hair and stared into her lifeless eyes. She was still beautiful and that last look of terror was captured in her eyes permanently, like a photograph.

There were tears in his eyes as he kissed her lips for the final time. Resting her head by her body he poured more gasoline onto it and tried to set it alight. Once again it wouldn't burn and he gave up.

He then put her headless body into another garbage bag, forced it into the case, and threw it as hard as he could into the larger of the two lakes. George Skiadopoulos watched without emotion as the suitcase slowly sank into the muddy waters and disappeared.

Picking up Julie's head, which was now burned beyond recognition, he put it in the trunk and set off for the last time to Kavala. Halfway there he stopped the car and threw the hacksaw, gas container and lighter into a field by the road.

It was nearly dawn when Skiadopoulos reached Kalmitsa Beach and stopped the Fiat by the cliffs that jut out over the Aegean Sea. In warmer weather the idyllic spot is a favorite for young lovers. But on this icy January night it was deserted.

It was here that Skiadopoulos cradled Julie's charred head before tossing it into the Aegean Sea far below, where he knew the strong currents would carry it far away from shore.

Turning back toward the car, he smiled as he noticed that "AGAPO," the Greek word for "love" had been scrawled on one of the gray rocks facing the sea.

He savored the thought that Julie would never, ever leave him.

CHAPTER SEVENTEEN

THE ALIBI

For the next two days George Skiadopoulos hid out in the new apartment he had taken with Julie. He showered and got rid of his clothes, which were stained in Julie's blood, and disposed of her passport and credit cards.

On Saturday he spent hours walking around the cobbled streets of Kavala, making sure he only went out after dark, so he wouldn't be seen by anyone he knew. He slowly concocted an alibi to explain Julie's disappearance so he could resume his life and then empty their joint account as soon as it was safe. That night he started calling his family and friends, telling them that he and Julie had reached Athens safely and would pick up her container from the docks on Monday morning.

On Sunday he drove the four hundred miles to Athens and began putting his alibi into place. In an elaborate charade, he would pretend that he and Julie had gone to Omonia Square in downtown Athens late Sunday night. Feeling hungry, she had gone off to a nearby Mc-

Donald's in the square while he made a telephone call to his family. When he went there to find her, she had disappeared.

At around midnight he began to make the first of a series of calls to establish his alibi. First he breathlessly telephoned his mother and grandmother in Kavala, asking if they had heard from Julie. Then he called his father in Athens, saying that Julie had disappeared and he was very worried. Taking the bait, Pavlos Skiadopoulos agreed to meet his son immediately and help him search for his fiancée.

Skiadopoulos met his father at the police station in Omonia Square, where they filed a missing persons report for Julie. Although the police were sympathetic enough, they did not take it too seriously. It was very common for people to vanish from the seedy transient area, which resembles the old Times Square in New York City, and most of them turned up eventually. They encouraged Skiadopoulos to search for his fiancée and let them know when she was found.

For the next few hours father and son went around Omonia Square showing Julie's picture to the staff at McDonald's and doing the rounds of the many late-night bars and fast-food joints. While his father comforted him, George Skiadopoulos seemed close to tears as he repeatedly asked everyone in the square if they had seen Julie.

Early Monday morning George arrived at the American Embassy to report Julie missing. The clerk on duty was also sympathetic but never took it any further, believing that they had probably had a lovers' tiff, that Julie had run off and would soon turn up.

That afternoon Skiadopoulos telephoned Susan White at her home in Moorestown, New Jersey, saying Julie was missing. It would be the first of many telephone calls Skiadopoulos would make to Julie's friend over the next two weeks.

"I was getting ready to take my son to school when he called," remembers Sue. "He said, 'I can't find her!' He was extremely panicky."

Skiadopoulos repeated his story of how they had gone to Athens to pick up her container and Julie had disappeared on the way to McDonald's.

"He was a very good actor," said Sue. "My first thought was that she took off and wanted to get away from him. I asked him if they had been fighting. I know Julie's temper and I could see her getting really pissed and storming out because of the phone calls. But George said they weren't fighting."

Skiadopoulos's elaborate alibi seemed plausible enough at first. He told Sue that Julie had two hundred dollars in cash and her credit cards in her purse, but that she had left her passport in the Fiat. He said she had been wearing a black dress, high heels and had her hair in a pony tail. He also told Sue that he had spoken to a policeman in Omonia Square who had seen Julie. But later the policeman could not be found.

Sue then asked him if he had checked their new apartment in Kavala to see if she'd gone back without telling him.

"Then George got really mad at me," said Sue. "He said he didn't have the keys."

As soon as she put down the telephone, Sue called Tim Nist and left a message on his telephone, asking him to call her. When he didn't return the call Sue telephoned again in the afternoon and this time Tim picked up. She told him that George had called, saying Julie had disappeared.

Tim's first thought was that his ex-wife had jumped on a plane and come home. But when he heard George's explanation of her disappearance, something didn't gel. It seemed inconceivable that she would not have taken her passport if she was planning to run away.

"I was a little concerned," said Tim. "I knew Julie was a resourceful girl and I'd never seen her fail at anything she wanted to do. I thought she'd told George to go to hell and left . . . but it was strange about the passport."

After he put down the phone, Tim called Julia Scully into his bedroom to tell her that Julie was missing. Julia's first thought was that Skiadopoulos had turned violent again and her daughter was hiding out somewhere for her own protection.

"I prayed a lot," said Julia. "I asked God to take me instead of Julie, because she's got a little girl."

Tim then telephoned the American Embassy in Greece but it was closed. So he called Tony Capella, asking him to use his political connections to try and discover what was going on.

"The minute Tim told me, I knew George had killed her," remembered Capella. "Based on what he tried doing to her mother, I knew. But I hoped I was wrong."

Capella then called his local Republican congressman and friend Rodney Freemanhausen, who agreed to write a letter to the American ambassador in Athens to get some action.

Later that day George Skiadopoulos called Sue White again. This time he sounded more worried than ever, saying he had spent the day in Omonia Square looking for Julie. His story had also changed. He now admitted that he and Julie had argued before she left for McDonald's.

*   *   *

At 8:15 p.m. on Monday night Tracey Allen was in her kitchen watching *Melrose Place* when she got a call from Tim, telling her about Julie. As soon as she heard George's story, she too was alarmed, knowing that Julie would never go anywhere without her passport. Although she had only met Sue White on a couple of occasions, she got her number from Tim and phoned her. By the end of their two-hour conversation both women had pledged to work together to find Julie. It would be the beginning of a close friendship and partnership that would ultimately bring Skiadopoulos to justice.

Ironically, when Tracey heard the news she was just about to send off Julie's bills to Greece; they were lying in a pile on her kitchen table. Tracey told Sue that she would monitor Julie's credit cards for usage, and access her account information to find out where she was.

"We knew that time was critical," said Tracey. "and prayed that there would be some kind of paper trail. Maybe she had checked into a hotel or there was a flight ticket to somewhere."

As Tracey had never met George during his six-week stay in New Jersey, it was decided that Sue would become the contact to him. She would have to be his friend and lull him into a false sense of security, until he made his mistake.

Active in many local social causes, Tracey Allen was a natural-born organizer, and she'd bring her valuable talent to the search for Julie. As a campus journalist for the Laurenceville College newspaper, she also had access to a network of contacts whom she put to work. She would also liaise with the Greek police and the American Embassy in Athens to try persuading them to search for Julie. That night she called all the Athens hospitals, in case Julie had been brought in.

Tracey set her alarm for 5:00 a.m. the following morning and started hitting the phones to Greece. Although she had never made an international call in her life, she soon found the American Embassy number and was put through to a woman named Christine, who already knew about Julie's disappearance.

She confirmed that Skiadopoulos had contacted them and the police about Julie and said he had already called several Athens TV stations for help. But as far as Tracey could ascertain George Skiadopoulos was the sole person actively searching for Julie.

"I told her that in our country George would be a suspect," said Tracey. "I was told, 'George is not under suspicion right now. He seems like a nice guy.'"

That day Tracey had the flu and called in sick, spending her time plotting out a strategy with Sue White. They agreed that the next time George called they would try and rattle him, by saying that they had now enlisted the help of powerful American politicians.

"We were hoping that he would make a critical mistake and we would catch him," said Tracey. "Maybe he was holding Julie hostage somewhere."

When George called a few hours later, Sue told him that the hunt for Julie was escalating and there were politicians involved. Skiadopoulos appeared happy at the news, begging Sue to tell Julie, if she called, that he loved her and wanted her to come back to him.

For the next few days Tracey called the American Embassy at least twice a day to monitor developments. But when she contacted the Athens police she was thwarted as no one spoke English. By amazing coincidence a freelancer at her job had been born in Kavala, and spoke the language perfectly. She agreed to act as translator and began calling the police every day, refusing to take a cent for the calls.

On Wednesday night Skiadopoulos called again and Sue lied, telling him that the FBI was now involved in the case. Although he said he was pleased that she had called in the FBI, Sue detected a slight panic in his voice as he told her he was returning to Kavala. Before he left, he promised to put up some missing posters in Omonia Square, offering a reward for information leading to Julie.

The following night Skiadopoulos called Sue to inform her that he had been mugged in Omonia Square by two unarmed men who had stolen his bag, containing Julie's passport and several photographs.

"Now we knew something was up," said Tracey. "He fell into our trap and panicked. Now I began to fear the worst."

Two days went by without any further calls from Skiadopoulos. Sue telephoned various members of his family in Kavala, but no one seemed to know where he was. When Tracey's translator called George's godmother in Kavala, she was told the family all loved Julie and were worried about her.

By this time Tracey and Sue were talking constantly, trying to come up with various theories to explain Julie's disappearance. Sue even wondered if her beautiful friend had been sold into white slavery or prostitution. "Our minds were running wild by now," explained Tracey.

On Saturday, January 15, deciding that there was little he could do to find his ex-wife, Tim Nist left for a previously booked week-long Caribbean cruise with a new girlfriend. Throughout that weekend Tracey and Sue became increasingly worried for Julie's safety as they made call after call to try locating George.

Early Monday morning Skiadopoulos was back in contact. He called Sue in a state of panic, trying to find out if Julie had said anything about their relationship in the days before she had gone missing.

"I remember thinking, 'There's something he's afraid of,'" said Sue. "He kept saying, 'Did she call you? Did she call you?' Something must have happened in the time he disappeared. He was now afraid that I had information that he didn't want me to have. Tracey and I wondered if he had disposed of her body during this time." As the week wore on Skiadopoulos called less and less often.

On Friday morning George walked into his bank in Kavala and tried to withdraw money from his joint account with Julie. When the bank manager told him that the American check for almost $90,000 had still not cleared and no funds were available, Skiadopoulos stormed out of the bank in a fury.

By now Julie's friends were so desperate that when Cheryl Chuplis suggested consulting a psychic, they agreed. Cheryl knew one named Gladys Ivey in Levittown, Pennsylvania, who was often called in by homicide detectives when their clues had dried up.

During a telephone consultation Ivey told Cheryl that it didn't look good for Julie.

"She said Julie was surrounded by water," remembered Chuplis. "She kept saying she was hurt and that she could see hands around her neck and that her legs are broken. This upset everybody and we just prayed it was not true."

Tracey Allen also called in a psychic who told her almost the exact same thing.

It was now two weeks since Skiadopoulos had killed Julie, and the arrogant former sailor was becoming more and more confident that he had committed the perfect murder.

On Friday, Tracey Allen's barrage of calls to the American Embassy finally paid off. Embassy officials alerted border patrols to watch out for Julie Scully and contacted several influential Greek television reporters, suggesting they do a story on her disappearance. That evening George Frimis, an on-air crime reporter from the top-rated Antenna television station, telephoned Skiadopoulos in Kavala to follow up.

"He said he wanted to talk to me," said Frimis. "We agreed to meet on Monday at the McDonald's in Omonia Square, where she had gone missing."

Independently, Tracey had also decided to use the American media, hoping to embarrass the Greek authorities into actively searching for Julie. She wanted to get the story out on the Associated Press (AP) international wire to "smoke out" Julie's captor, so she decided to write a press release. She knew it was vital not to alarm George and make him think they suspected him, so she drafted a carefully worded release, strong enough to provoke coverage from the media, but not a flight attempt by Skiadopoulos.

January 23, 1999
FOR IMMEDIATE RELEASE

JULIE SCULLY (FORMERLY JULIE NIST), AGE 31, OF MANSFIELD, NEW JERSEY: RE-PORTED MISSING IN ATHENS, GREECE, JANUARY 10

Ms. Scully, former Page 6 Girl for the *Trentonian* newspaper in New Jersey, disappeared in Athens

Greece, on January 10. Her boyfriend, George Skiadopoulos who is a resident of Greece, reported the following.

On January 10 at midnight, Mr. Skiadopoulos and Ms. Scully arrived in Athens from the town of Kavala. They were there to visit family, and pick up furniture. Mr. Skiadopoulos also said they were there to get married.

Upon arrival in Athens, the couple had an argument, according to Mr. Skiadopoulos. He wanted to make a phone call, and Ms. Scully wanted to get something to eat. They split up. Mr. Skiadopoulos took the car to a pay phone, and Ms. Scully started on a seven-minute walk to the McDonald's. This was only the second time Ms. Scully had been in Athens, and she did not speak the language. She did not take her passport with her.

After making his phone call, Mr. Skiadopoulos drove to McDonald's. Ms. Scully was not there, and no one in the restaurant had seen her. She vanished.

Mr. Skiadopoulos reported her missing to the police and the American Embassy, and the next day alerted her family.

An Athens police officer reported to Mr. Skiadopoulos that he had seen Ms. Scully walking [near Omonia Square]. The family has tried to find the officer, but he has not reported to the Embassy, and Mr. Skiadopoulos has not yet revealed his name to the family.

The Embassy alerted the border on January 22 to keep an eye out for Ms. Scully, and they will begin advertising soon. Police are looking into her mysterious disappearance. The Embassy and the Police believe that there was foul play.

The last contact from Ms. Scully to the family was on January 6. At that time, Ms. Scully reported that she was very unhappy and wanted to come home. Ms. Scully has a three-year-old daughter who misses her terribly. She keeps asking for her mommy, and the family is saddened that this small child may have lost her mother.

On Saturday morning Tim Nist returned from his cruise and gave Tracey the go-ahead to fax out the release to thirty newspapers and ten television stations on the East Coast.

"At noon that day my phone began to ring," she said, "and it didn't stop until 9:00 p.m. when I finally took it off the hook."

CHAPTER EIGHTEEN

OUTSMARTED

At nine o'clock on Saturday morning the city editor of *The Trentonian*, Paul Micole, picked Tracey Allen's press release off the fax machine and knew he had a big story on his hands. It was only three months since the "What Are They Doing Now?" feature on Julie had appeared, so he immediately called Eric Ladley, who had conducted the interview, telling him to come straight into the office.

"I was working the weekend cops' beat," said Ladley. "When Paul told me she was missing in Greece, my first thought was, 'What the hell is she doing there?'"

When Ladley read the press release he thought it "weird" as Skiadopoulos's story did not add up. He also carefully noted Tracey's nuances, which peppered the release.

"She said that Mr. Skiadopoulos claimed they were going to get married, which made it sound like they weren't," said Ladley. "Right away I wondered if she was in trouble," he said.

He then drove to Mansfield Township to interview Tim Nist and Julie's mother; he also spoke to Tracey Allen and Sue White by phone. By the time he returned to *The Trentonian*, Ladley was certain that something terrible had happened to Julie.

The following day *The Trentonian* devoted the entire front page to Julie's disappearance. With a banner headline, "Page 6 Model Mystery," the editors saved her old swimsuit shots for page three, tastefully putting a picture of Julie fully dressed in a lilac bridesmaid's gown—taken at Tracey Allen's wedding a year earlier—on the front.

Ladley's story, headlined "Vanishing Act," reported that Julie's friends were fearful for her safety.

"We haven't been sleeping," Tracey was quoted as saying. "She's a beautiful, wonderful girl and I hope to God we get her back alive."

Julia Scully, who would become one of Ladley's best sources in the story, wasn't afraid to shoot from the hip and voice her views on Skiadopoulos. "He is possessive, arrogant and stupid," stated Julie's mother. "He is like an addiction!"

By the time Tim Nist arrived at his gym on Sunday morning, everybody knew about Julie's disappearance and offered their support. During his work-out he struck up a conversation with a lieutenant he knew from the Trenton Police Department, who warned him to be extremely careful with how he dealt with the press.

The lieutenant told Tim that if George's alibi stuck, he could find himself the prime suspect.

"He said the more you talk, the more trouble you're going to be in," said Tim.

A few hours later the story hit the AP wires, and it made several Athens newspapers later that day. When George Skiadopoulos read it he was furious and called Sue White to complain about the press release.

"Everybody's against me!" he screamed down the phone to New Jersey. "Everybody's looking at me funny!"

By Monday morning, the Greek authorities were taking Julie's disappearance seriously and assigned the case to the Espalia Security Police's homicide squad. Since the AP story had broken the search was gathering momentum on both continents.

Eric Ladley was now in regular contact with the AP Athens bureau chief, Brian Murphy, who was a New Jersey native. From now on they would work the story together.

It was late morning when Antenna Television news reporter George Frimis walked into McDonald's in Omonia Square to find Skiadopoulos already there waiting. For the next three hours the well-groomed young journalist would try and persuade him to give an on-camera interview.

Dressed casually in a black leather jacket with a white shirt and carrying a blue plastic shoulder bag, Skiadopoulos appeared relaxed and genuinely concerned about the fate of his fiancée. He told Frimis how he had met Julie on the Galaxy and the story of how their love affair had developed.

"We spoke for a very long time," said Frimis. "At first he only wanted to give me her picture but I wanted him to go on camera."

At one point Skiadopoulos asked Frimis to wait a minute while he got something outside in the square.

Half an hour later he returned to McDonald's, saying that he had decided to do an on-camera interview.

"He was probably rehearsing what he was going to say," said Frimis. "Perfecting his alibi."

When the camera crew arrived from the studio, located in a north Athens suburb, Skiadopoulos repeated the story of Julie's disappearance as the video camera rolled. Throughout the interview he would constantly refer to Julie as "the woman," a point which wasn't lost on the experienced crime reporter.

"A thirty-year-old woman, an American citizen who did not speak Greek, disappeared in a very mysterious way," he began, waving his hands for extra emphasis. "We came from Kavala with the intention of getting married in Athens and to pick up the woman's things which had been shipped from America."

But what really aroused Frimis's suspicions was Skiadopoulos's claim that he had been robbed of her passport. First he said that the men had not been armed and then during the interview he changed his story, saying that they had guns.

"I realized there was something wrong with his story," said Frimis. "And by the time we aired the interview on the late news that night, I knew he was the one. So I deliberately left question marks open in the report."

After the story aired, Frimis also got a call from the Athens AP deputy bureau chief Patrick Quinn, who had seen the interview and thought it "bizarre." The Boston-born journalist, whose biting wit and tenacity had made him a legend during his decade-long assignment in Athens, told Frimis he thought there were "humungous holes" in Skiadopoulos's story.

"I told Frimis, 'It stinks,'" said Quinn. "He agreed

and we sat there discussing all the holes in this guy's story. I told him he should go to the police straight away."

Frimis put down the phone and called a detective he knew in Espalia, the crack homicide division at Athens police headquarters. He gave him Skiadopoulos's phone number in Athens. Within the hour George was on the phone, telling Frimis that he had just been ordered to report to police headquarters the following day.

"George is a good actor," said Frimis. "He said it was a good sign that they were taking Julie's disappearance seriously and he was only too pleased to be of help."

Five thousand miles away in New Jersey, Tim Nist had no idea that the story was gaining momentum in Greece. On the advice of a friend he had hired an Athens-based private investigator, though they still had not signed an agreement.

Nist was also concerned that *The Trentonian* had not run a story that day on Julie, so he called Eric Ladley and invited him to the house, saying that he had vital new information on Julie. As they sat down on his comfortable couch in the front room, Tim told the reporter how George had been arrested for trying to strangle Julie's mother. He also mentioned that his ex-wife had taken more than one hundred thousand dollars over to Greece.

But when Ladley began interviewing Julia about the attack, Tracey Allen arrived at the house and tried to run interference.

"Tracey wanted to keep a lid on it," said Ladley. "She was leery about what went into the paper. She didn't want this in, she didn't want that in. But Julie's mom didn't care. She didn't hold anything back."

CHAPTER NINETEEN

THE CONFESSION

On Tuesday, January 26, George Skiadopoulos calmly walked into the Espalia police headquarters in downtown Athens. It had now been sixteen days since he had first reported Julie missing and Skiadopoulos felt confident as he walked up to the front desk. He arrogantly believed that he had already outsmarted the media, so homicide detectives should pose few problems.

The desk sergeant told him to wait in a room where he was joined, a few minutes later, by Espalia's chief interrogator, Inspector Vasilus Tiapourdoras. The tough Athens detective had seen the video of Skiadopoulos's TV interview and was very suspicious. Now he was going for a full confession.

At first Skiadopoulos seemed unruffled as he repeated his well-rehearsed alibi. But when the inspector began closely questioning him about Julie's passport, he began to contradict himself and get flustered. The harder In-

spector Tiapourdoras probed, the more agitated Skiadopoulos became.

After four hours of intense questioning Skiadopoulos
finally broke down, confessing that he had killed Julie
and then decapitated her in a bizarre act of passion.

"He was sobbing," said journalist Panos Somboulos,
known as the dean of Greek crime reporters, who was
to have interviewed Skiadopoulos the following day.
"He said, 'I will tell you everything.' "

At about seven o'clock Tiapourdoras turned on a tape
recorder as George Skiadopoulos started his rambling
and often emotional confession.

"Julie did not disappear," he began. "I am telling you
lies and I have lied up to now. I killed her with my own
hands. I strangled her."

Then Skiadopoulos told the detective how he had first
met Julie aboard the Galaxy, saying that they had had a
mutual attraction. After the end of the cruise, he said,
Julie had convinced her husband to go on a second one
so she and George could see one another again.

"During the voyage Julie made it clear that she
wanted to have a relationship with me," he said. "It was
consummated. Initially I felt guilty because she was married and had a three-year-old child. I was also having a
relationship with a Dutch woman who worked on the
ship."

Skiadopoulos then described the halcyon dawn of
their affair, and how Julie had flown to Puerto Rico the
previous March for a rendezvous with him.

"That day we spoke seriously about our relationship,"
he said. "She told me about the problems she was having
with her husband and how indifferent he was toward her.

She said she was considering a separation so we could live together."

Skiadopoulos said he had warned Julie not to walk out of her marriage without giving it a great deal of thought, claiming that he did not want to cause their divorce.

He then described their two weeks together on the Galaxy as "a period of intense happiness," outlining how he had quit his job to live with Julie in Mansfield Township. But he carefully omitted his arrest after the attack on Julie's mother or any explanation of why he had to leave America.

He told Tiapourdoras about Julie's first trip to Greece three months earlier, and how they planned to get married. When he took Julie to Kavala to meet his family for the first time, she was very happy.

But Skiadopoulos said everything changed when she returned to Greece in early December.

"She constantly criticized me for the different attitudes between Greece and the United States," he explained. "Julie was used to a different way of life and every day she would emphasize the differences. I became very concerned about the future of our relationship.

"I tried to think logically, putting aside my own feelings, which were pure and strong. We discussed the problems that we might face in the future, but Julie assured me that she would adapt to living in Greece eventually. But it was not happening."

Skiadopoulos now claimed that it was *he* who wanted Julie to return to America while he did his military service. According to Skiadopoulos, it was Julie who refused, saying that it was too long for them to be apart. Then Skiadopoulos said he offered to skip the army and run off to America. But Julie said it wasn't a good idea as he wouldn't have a green card and would be there illegally.

"I could not find a solution to the problem so I decided it would be better for us to separate and Julie return back to the United States," said Skiadopoulos. "But Julie would not accept it."

In Skiadopoulos's rather unconvincing motive for murdering Julie, he claimed that initially he only wanted to hit her, so she would leave him.

"Julie had told me that she would never allow a boyfriend to beat her," said Skiadopoulos. "I thought that if I was violent it would destroy all the feelings that she had for me, and she would go back to America. So I tried to find the right time to justify my action to hit her, so she would not understand my true intentions."

At this point he lapsed into floods of tears and the inspector had to halt the confession while Skiadopoulos composed himself.

Continuing, Skiadopoulos said he decided to act on Friday, January 8, while they were driving to Athens to collect her belongings. A few miles out of Kavala, Julie had asked him why he was so sad.

"I told her again the problems I saw in our relationship," he said. "and I asked her to separate. She wouldn't accept it and we started arguing. During the fight I stopped on a side road and drove onto a dirt track. I thought it would be the opportunity to hit her, so I grabbed her by the throat and started shaking her. She was sitting next to me in the passenger seat and I turned towards her and grabbed her by the neck.

"She started yelling, 'What are you doing!' I clouded up. I became scared and without wanting to I grabbed her harder so she wouldn't scream. Two or three minutes later I let her go and I realized it was too late because she was dead. I tried to revive her but I could not."

After killing Julie, Skiadopoulos said, he could no longer think logically. He just knew instinctively that he must get rid of her body.

"Because we met at sea I considered burning her body and then tossing her ashes into the [Aegean Sea] and then committing suicide. I brought Julie down from the car and put her in the trunk and went to the gas station in Nea Peramos. I didn't have a gas container so I went to another station where I bought a four-liter container.

"I drove back on the national road from Kavala to Salonika, trying to find a secluded, out-of-the-way spot to burn the body. Before I got to the place where I had killed Julie, just past the one-hundred-and-thirty-second kilometer signpost, I turned right onto a dirt road and I continued for about fifty meters.

"I saw that there were two small lakes next to each other and I stopped. I took out Julie's corpse from the trunk and I left it about five meters from the second lake. Then I doused her with gasoline and set her on fire. Her clothes caught alight but her body wasn't burning despite the fact that I kept on pouring the gas.

"The fire went out and then I thought of tossing her into the lake-swamp. Initially I moved her corpse so I could hide it. But I changed my mind and put it in the trunk of the car.

"I took off and went to my grandmother's house as she wasn't at home at the time. I took a large black suitcase and put it in the car and left to go back to the lakes. By now it was about midnight. When I got there I took the body out of the trunk and I tried to put it in the suitcase. It wouldn't fit in and her head wouldn't go inside.

"Then I remembered that my grandmother had an iron hacksaw at her house. I decided to get it so I could cut off her head.

"I left the suitcase with the corpse near my grandmother's house and took the hacksaw from the house. I drove back to the same spot without seeing anyone I knew on the way. When I got to the lake I took her corpse from the suitcase. I cut off her head at the height of the neck and I tried again to burn her body so she would be ashes.

"Again it wouldn't burn so I put the body in the suitcase and closed it. Then I tossed it into the lake. I watched as the suitcase sunk into the muddy waters. I put the head in the trunk, intending to toss it into the sea.

"Then I started back to Kavala but about halfway to Kavala I stopped and threw away the saw, the gas canister and the lighter. I was in a haze and I can't remember where I tossed it on the road.

"I tossed the head over the cliffs at Kalamitza beach, just outside Kavala. The head was burned and there was practically no skin left. I was almost beside myself and I didn't know what I was doing from the moment I realized Julie was dead."

At the end of his dramatic confession, Skiadopoulos told the detective that he had attempted suicide three times since the murder: by cutting his wrists, taking an overdose of Julie's pills, and by shooting himself with a gun he had bought in a Salonika hunting store.

"I went to an isolated area in Kavala and tried to shoot myself dead. But I missed and only sustained a small injury to my head," he explained.

At about 10:00 p.m. George Skiadopoulos was handcuffed and led out of the back entrance of police headquarters by four detectives and placed in a waiting car. There they were joined by the head of Espalia, General Pavlos Roubis. Crime reporter Panos Somboulos had also been invited alone.

Skiadopoulos had finally agreed to lead the detectives to Julie's headless body. But the weather was so foggy that night that Olympic Airways had suspended all flights north. They would have to drive through the night to reach Kavala by daybreak.

As the convoy of detectives, forensic experts and a pathologist left Athens for the seven-hour drive to Kavala, Patrick Quinn of AP was dining with some friends in a restaurant. In the middle of the meal he received a call from his police reporter with the dramatic news that Skiadopoulos had confessed.

"Patrick, he's cut her into a hundred pieces," yelled the reporter, barely able to contain himself. "They're driving up to Kavala right now to find the body."

Quinn immediately dashed out of the restaurant and drove straight to the AP office on Amalias Street, in the shadows of the Greek Parliament Building. He started calling his police contacts and within an hour the sensational story of George's confession had moved on the AP wire.

It was 5:35 p.m. in New Jersey when Eric Ladley read Quinn's story in stunned disbelief. His adrenaline pumping, he called Tim Nist and broke the news of Skiadopoulos's confession and how the police were now driving to Kavala to find Julie's body. Ladley requested an interview and Tim told him to come straight over.

After hearing the news, Tim went up to his office to call his local Congressman Chris Smith to find out exactly what was happening. He made sure that Julie's mother, who was baby-sitting Katie, didn't hear the conversation until the report could be verified.

Congressman Smith, who is chairman of the subcommittee for International Operations and Human Rights, immediately faxed an urgent letter to the American Ambassador in Athens, R. Nicholas Burns, asking him to personally intervene.

"The most recent Associated Press story reports that Ms. Scully's remains may be located near the town of Kavala, the hometown of Mr. Skiadopoulos," wrote Smith. "Mr. Nist and Ms. Scully's family are devastated by these reports and have been tormented by their inability to receive updated, reliable information from the State Department."

When Eric Ladley arrived at Mansfield Road he found an obviously shocked Tim, cooking supper and trying to act like nothing was wrong. Little Katie was running around with her favorite stuffed toy bear, totally unaware of the drama that was unfolding around her.

Then Tim ushered Ladley out of the house so he could read the AP story.

"Tim said he wasn't surprised but he still seemed pretty stunned by it," said Ladley. "You could tell his voice was trembling but he didn't cry. But he didn't want me talking to Mrs. Scully or Katie until we knew more."

Tim went back inside the house to find Katie and her grandmother sitting at the kitchen table eating dinner. He deliberately sat with his back to them so they wouldn't see how upset he was.

"By this time I was crying," said Nist. "I was trying not to say anything. All I could think of is that I wish I'd been there to protect Julie."

Then the phone rang and Tim went upstairs to answer

it. On the other end was AP's Trenton bureau chief Meredith Burney, who wanted an interview. From now on Tim would be besieged by journalists twenty four hours a day, as the full horror of what Skiadopoulos had done to Julie emerged.

Trying to calm his nerves, Tim started drinking beer after beer as he called all Julie's friends to tell them the grim news. And, realizing that it was only a matter of time before Julie's mother found out, he came downstairs and took Julia out into the garden and told her about George's confession and how he was even now taking police to the body.

"So he killed her!" declared Julia. "I knew he would and I warned her. I told her not to trust him but she said, 'Mom, you read too many novels.' "

CHAPTER TWENTY

FOUND

At five o'clock on Wednesday morning, George Skia-dopoulos led a convoy of police cars to the dirty swamp where he had dumped Julie's body, nineteen days earlier. It was still dark and near freezing as they parked beside the man-made lake. They were then joined by a team of police divers who would begin their search as soon as the sun came up.

The mists were rising off the icy water as the divers entered the dense, muddy lake, using flashlights to locate the suitcase containing Julie's remains. Now under sui-cide watch, Skiadopoulos stood handcuffed to a detec-tive by the side of the lake, his head bowed. There was not a flicker of emotion on his face as he watched the search for his fiancée's remains, and he did not utter one word.

Two hours later the divers located the suitcase under five feet of water and brought it to the surface. Skiado-poulos, who had been silent up to now, began to cry as he watched the filthy black case being carried out by a diver and placed by the side of the lake.

Then the police ushered the reporters and photographers away as they prepared to open it and see what was inside. Although the experienced detectives were well acquainted with death, nothing had prepared them for what they would find.

There was a terrible shudder as the suitcase was opened to reveal Julie's naked headless body inside. It was in the fetal position, shrouded in a black garbage bag and newspapers.

"It was a very emotional moment which no one who was there will ever forget," said Panos Somboulos. "She had been beheaded but her body was perfectly preserved because of the freezing temperatures. Even as a corpse you could tell she had been a very beautiful woman."

As the police began to pry her body out of the suitcase, Skiadopoulos began mumbling unintelligibly to himself, his eyes glazing over with tears. When a detective asked him what he had done with Julie's head, he slowly pointed towards Kavala, saying he'd thrown it in the sea. "So I can always be with her," he muttered.

Julie's body was then placed on a stretcher and carried to a bright red ambulance that would take it to the airport, where it would be flown to Athens for autopsy.

The police now declared the whole area a crime scene, as they began searching the swamp for forensic evidence. They were seeking traces of hair, nails and anything else that could be used in the murder investigation. They also began dusting down the white Fiat Punto for fingerprints.

Finally a policeman carried away the empty suitcase, which dripped Julie's blood onto the muddy ground below.

At 9:30 a.m. the Greek police officially notified the American Embassy of Julie's death and Skiadopoulos's arrest for her murder. As he was taken to the police station in Kavala to be formally charged, the divers moved to Kalamitza Beach, where they would spend the next three days in a futile search for her head.

Julia Scully had hardly slept a wink after hearing about George's confession. She had finally dozed off, leaving the television by her bed in the basement tuned to a news station. At about 4:00 a.m. Eastern Standard Time, she awoke during a news bulletin to hear a report that Julie's headless body had been found.

"I couldn't believe he cut off her head," sobbed Julia, three months later. "I was in shock. I mean, I heard it on the television!"

Julia then rushed upstairs to the TV room where Tim was asleep on a couch. She woke him up and asked if he knew anything about Julie's decapitation.

"I turned on the news," said Tim. "Oh God! And there it is. 'The headless body of Julie Scully . . .' "

Tim and Julia both collapsed into each other's arms sobbing, as they absorbed the full horror of what had happened. But Nist managed to compose himself, telling his ex-mother-in-law that they had to be strong for Katie, who would be up soon.

Then Tim got a call from the Athens private investigator, claiming responsibility for finding Julie's body, and demanding his fee. Nist was so angry at his insensitivity that he slammed down the phone.

By this time a media circus was gathering on Tim's front lawn, as scores of television crews, reporters and photographers started ringing the front bell requesting interviews. Tim came out briefly for what he later called "the global Julie network," promising he would talk to them later that morning.

At 9:00 a.m. Tim got a call from Suzanne Payne, Chief of American Services for the Consular Section in the U.S. Embassy in Athens, confirming that Julie's body had been found. Payne said that the press release issued by the Greek police contained such "horrible" details that she was reluctant to fax it without talking to him first. The press release was a condensed version of George Skiadopoulos's confession the day before, but it ended with the horrifying discovery a few hours earlier. Tim asked her to read the statement to him before faxing it.

"Today, in the morning hours, Police officers traveled to the area of Kavala, and based on information provided by the perpetrator, they found at the 132nd kilometer [sign] between Thessaloniki and Kavala, in a seventy-square-meter lake, at a depth of 1.5 meters, in a suitcase, the nude and decapitated body of the unfortunate woman. The search continues for the head and other evidence."

As soon as he received the fax from Greece, Tim took it into the kitchen, where Julia was making breakfast for Katie. Julie's mother was now on automatic; the full shock of what had happened to her daughter would take weeks to sink in.

"I said, 'I don't know if you want to read this,' " said Nist. "She said she did, so I gave it to her. It was a terrible moment."

Within hours of the discovery of Julie's body, Congressman Chris Smith wrote a letter to the Greek Ambassador in Washington D.C., Alexander Philon, saying that the future of good relations between the two countries required that "this tragic case be judiciously and expeditiously resolved."

"I would also like to convey to you the importance of justice being served on behalf of Ms. Scully. She has left behind a daughter, her parents, family and numerous friends," said the letter.

All through the morning, Julie's friends arrived one by one to comfort Tim and Julia. For the next three days they would bond together in an emotional and often tearful vigil for Julie. Some of Julie's friends felt guilty for distancing themselves from her in the final months of her life. Again and again they would relive the good times they had all once shared, with everyone half-expecting Julie to walk in through the front door, a big smile on her face, saying everything was all right. The cold, hard fact of her impossibly cruel murder by the man she had loved seemed surreal and beyond belief.

"It was the worst day of my life," said Tracey Allen, who had been up all night praying for Julie. "It was a nightmare."

Julie's brother John was on active duty aboard a submarine off the coast of Georgia, so the American Red Cross was alerted to radio him the news. It would be two weeks before he was able to get off the submarine and fly back to his family.

"I got a short radio message [the day they found her]," said John Scully. "All I knew was that she was murdered in Kavala and the subject was apprehended. I was very shocked and sad for my sister."

Julie's father didn't even know she had gone to Greece until he heard from his twin brother Joseph, a week after she had gone missing. Then he received a call from Tracey Allen, who faxed the press release from the Greek police about Julie's murder.

JOHN GLATT

"I was distraught," said Scully. "I was hoping it was somebody else."

Scully was so upset that he took three days off work and had to go to the doctor to get a prescription to calm him down.

"I was in rough shape," he said. "You never realize how much you can miss a child until they're gone."

When Tony Capella heard that they had found Julie's mutilated body, he drove straight to Tim's house, offering to accompany him to Greece to sort out Julie's affairs and help bring her body back to New Jersey. As Tim's passport was out of date, Congressman Chris Smith used his influence to cut through bureaucratic red tape, and Tim drove to Philadelphia that very day to collect it.

"I didn't really want to go to Greece, but there was no one else," said Tim. "I wasn't married to Julie anymore but I knew I'd have to be the one to go and bring her home."

On Thursday morning George Skiadopoulos was taken in handcuffs to the prosecutor's office in Kavala for arraignment. Wearing sunglasses, jeans, and a raincoat, he looked dazed as the head of the Espalia security police, General Pavlos Roubis, led him through a gauntlet of TV camera crews, reporters and curiosity-seekers, and into a waiting car.

As the reporters rushed towards him, hurling questions, Skiadopoulos mumbled, "I regret this," as he pushed his raincoat over his face to prevent his picture being taken.

On arrival at the prosecutor's office, Skiadopoulos was met by his new defense lawyer, Sakis Kehagloglou, who had been hired by his father. One of the most prominent lawyers in Greece, the Athens-based Kehagilou studied law in Washington, D.C., before coming back to Greece to practice.

"George's father called me," he said. "I considered it a very interesting case. A very interesting story. But the boy is not crazy. He had a bad moment."

Apart from Kehagloglou, Pavlos Skiadopoulos had also hired a local attorney in Kavala to help defend his son.

Later that morning the Kavala prosecutor Dimitris Papageorgiou officially charged Skiadopoulos with the premeditated murder of Julie Scully, desecrating her body, and lying to police. As the Greek death penalty was abolished in 1994, Skiadopoulos only faced a maximum twenty-five years in prison if convicted.

After seeing her son for the first time since his arrest, Simos Skiadopoulos came out of the prosecutor's office in a state of shock. With tears pouring down her cheeks, she told a Greek television reporter that she couldn't believe what her son had done.

"My son has repented," she said. "We loved the girl very much and I don't know why he did it. I want to give him my moral support as a mother. He is very disappointed and I just can't believe my son is a murderer. What else can I say?"

His grandmother, Tiriaki Papadopoulou also told reporters that she couldn't believe what had happened, saying, "They were so happy."

The only other family member Skiadopoulos would agree to see that day was his uncle, Thanasis Bozinis, who spoke to reporters as he came out of the jail.

"He's doing terrible," said Bozinis, who said there were police in the cell when he saw his nephew. "My personal opinion is that he doesn't know he's in jail. He thinks he's in a room. He doesn't know what he's done. I asked him if he was eating well, sleeping well, and he would not answer. He seemed lost and displaced. I asked him if he knew where Julie was and he did not answer. I asked him if he knew what happened and why he was there, and he kept saying, 'I don't know. I don't know. I don't know.' "

Soon after visiting her son, Simos Skiadopoulos was reported as having suffered a mild stroke and his father Pavlos was said to be heavily tranquilized. When he was contacted by AP, Pavlos Skiadopoulos said he was very sick, adding: "I can't understand. I am very sorry for Julie and her family."

Later that day the Kavala coroner, Phillipos Koutaki, held a press conference and said that, as Skiadopoulos had cut off Julie's head at the base of the neck, he could not categorically state that she had died from strangulation. He also called the Trenton Police Department, requesting DNA samples from Julia, Katie and Julie's father, so the body could be officially identified under Greek law.

As George Skiadopoulos was being arraigned, two suitcases from America arrived at his godmother's apartment. Inside were Julie's wedding dress and an assortment of cards and gifts from her family and friends.

CHAPTER TWENTY-ONE

FALLOUT

On Thursday, Julie Scully's horrific murder made the front page of newspapers all over America and Greece. The *New York Post* headline screamed: "Greek Tragedy: Jealous Lover Strangles, Burns and Beheads N.J. Beauty," while the *Philadelphia Inquirer* was slightly more restrained with, "In Greece, Her Dream of Love Ends in Death."

The media coverage in Greece was even more sensational, as the Athens police called it *the* worst crime in living memory. All the Greek television stations ran extensive news reports, portraying George Skiadopoulos as an inhuman monster. And the police mug shot, showing Skiadopoulos looking punchy with one eye almost closed, fitted the description perfectly.

Ethnos, carried Panos Somboulos's story containing Skiadopoulos's complete confession, with the headline "Erotic Passion Leads to Horrific Crime," while its rival

Fania trumpeted, "I Sent Her to the Sea Where I had Fallen in Love With Her."

Journalists at *The Trentonian*—who ran Julia Scully's anguished quote, "TEAR HIM TO PIECES" on Thursday's front page—now found themselves in the tricky position of being an integral part of the story they had to report. Realizing how sensitive the savage killing of the paper's best-known Page 6 model would be, publisher Dave Bonfield instructed his staff not to talk to the press, and issued a statement expressing the paper's sympathy to the Scully family.

"A lot of the media deluged us," said Bonfield. "I didn't want anyone to think we were trying to trade on it. We treated it as a news story but I didn't want to try and publicize it and make it anything more than it really was, which was a sad and tragic story."

But it was difficult for his reporters working on the story to be coldly objective, as many of them had known Julie and liked her. It was the biggest story Eric Ladley had ever worked on and although it was "exhilarating," he also found it "weird," having interviewed Julie just before her first trip to Greece.

That morning Tracey Allen turned on her radio to find WPST-FM (101.5) listeners hotly debating Julie's death. She became angrier and angrier as she heard a procession of callers criticizing Julie, saying they couldn't imagine how a mother could ever leave her child for another man.

"And it really pissed me off," said Tracey. "I was going to call the radio station to scream and yell at them. They were saying such terrible things about Julie. One thing I have learned is that you can never judge somebody until you walk a mile in their shoes."

*   *   *

That afternoon a Trenton police nurse arrived at Mansfield Road to take blood samples from Katie and her grandmother for DNA tests. The three-year-old girl, who still had no idea that her mother would never be coming home, became confused as the nurse brought a needle to take a sample of her blood. Although her father tried to pretend it was a nice game she could play, somehow Katie knew there was something wrong.

"I still don't know how I'm going to tell her," said Tim. "It will be hard."

As police divers continued their search for Julie's head in the freezing waters of the Aegean, Tim Nist flew into Athens with Tony Capella to find that he had become a celebrity. After landing at the airport on Sunday afternoon, after a twelve-hour flight with a Rome stop-over, they were whisked through customs to be greeted by the blinding camera lights of the Greek press and TV networks.

In the airport lobby, Tim gave an impromptu press conference to the crowd of reporters when he felt someone nudging his arm. He turned around to see the private investigator who had claimed responsibility for Skiadopoulos's arrest, displaying his card. Tim ignored the man, who wanted to be paid and would pester Nist throughout his stay in Greece.

Then Suzanne Payne, from the American Embassy, took charge, rushing Tim and Tony past the jostling paparazzi and into a limousine, which would take them to the Grand Britannia Hotel, in the center of Athens. For the next three days Nist would be continually harassed by reporters, looking for new angles in what had become the biggest murder story in many years.

"This is bigger than O.J.," Nist told the *Philadelphia*

Daily News in an interview from his hotel room that night.

Tim Nist's agenda in Greece was to sort out Julie's affairs and then bring her body back to New Jersey for a proper funeral. He also wanted to see Skiadopoulos face-to-face in the Kavala jail, to ask him why he had killed Julie and what he had done with her head.

In the wake of Julie's death Tim had been appointed the executor of her estate, and he needed to account for the $100,000 Julie had taken to Greece with her.

A few days earlier the Athens News Service had carried an unsubstantiated report that Skiadopoulos had withdrawn $80,000 from the joint bank account the day after the murder. Yet another report alleged that George's father had taken the money. After hearing the rumors Tim had called the Bank of Greece in Kavala and was told that the money was still there in the account.

"To the Greek press I was riding in there as some sort of savior," said Tim. "They seemed to have forgotten we were divorced."

On Monday morning Tim went to police headquarters and, using an interpreter, gave a four-hour deposition about his marriage with Julie and what he knew about George Skiadopoulos. After he finished he came out of the third-floor homicide division offices to find the Greek private investigator waiting for him. Tim angrily told him he wasn't getting a cent, as the contract he had faxed arrived twelve hours after Julie's body was discovered and had never been signed.

Then Nist and Capella went to the American Embassy where they met Ambassador Burns, who asked them not to speak to the press. Tim refused, telling the ambassador that he couldn't "ignore" the media as he needed them and didn't want to alienate their enemy.

As Tim left, the ambassador gave him the suitcases containing Julie's personal effects. But all the expensive jewelry she had brought to Greece and many other of her items had disappeared.

"That was tough," said Tim. "I said 'Tony, 'I just can't do this.' So Tony went through her stuff and came back crying."

Making it even harder were the reporters and paparazzi who had discovered where Nist was staying and staked out the hotel twenty-four hours a day. Finally, after several "group screaming matches," Tim laid down the ground rules for interviews, only speaking to one reporter at a time.

Tim was also upset about what he considered the cheap, sensational coverage by the Greek newspapers and resolved to emphasize Julie as a real person.

"I felt they didn't know anything about Julie here," he said. "I see all this stuff on TV with the bikini pictures and I wanted them to know the *real* Julie."

On Tuesday the Greek police told Tim that they wouldn't release Julie's body until the DNA testing to officially identify her had been completed. They were now also asking for a blood test from Julie's father to be flown over in addition to Katie's and Julia's, which had been shipped UPS. It was expected to be at least ten days before the complete results came in.

"I called the FBI in Athens and laid into the guy," said Nist. "I said, 'You've got a mother, a daughter and that's a straight line. You can't miss on that.' I mean, they're getting O.J. from a blot of blood lying in a driveway for eight hours."

Finally on Thursday, February 4, a disappointed Tim Nist and Tony Capella flew back to America, pledging to return to Greece once the authorities released Julie's remains.

Two days earlier, George Skiadopoulos had been brought in before an investigating magistrate in Kavala to give a deposition. He continually broke down in tears as he admitted killing Julie, but denied it was premeditated.

Once again his story had changed. He now told the magistrate that Julie had refused to marry him after they got a marriage license in Kavala. He had become so upset that he then killed her.

His lawyer Sakis Kehagioglou told reporters outside the court that he was considering an insanity plea for his client.

"It look like there are psychological problems," he said.

On Monday, February 1, Skiadopoulos was examined by court-ordered psychiatrist Dr. Alexandros Hourmouziadis, to determine whether he was insane. After asking him about Julie's murder and giving him some standard tests, the doctor declared Skiadopoulos sane and fit to stand trial. Kehagioglou immediately requested that his client be tested by a second psychiatrist and the magistrate agreed.

Five days later, Skiadopoulos gave a dramatic interview from his jail cell to *Ta Nea*, the biggest circulation newspaper in Greece. He told the paper that if he were the presiding judge, he would condemn himself to death.

"The only punishment I deserve is death," declared Skiadopoulos, fully aware that Greece no longer had a death penalty.

When Julia Scully heard about Skiadopoulos's jailhouse interview she was furious.

"He's a coward, isn't he?" she told *The Trentonian*'s Eric Ladley. "There is no punishment out there that can justify what he did. He says he loved my daughter. How can he do what he did to her body and claim that he loves her?

"Does he deserve to die? I don't think so. He deserves to live forever and ever. George, you took my granddaughter's mother away."

Her daughter's murder had a terrible effect on Julia Scully, who moved into Tim's house to look after Katie. After her final, bitter telephone conversation with Julie, she felt guilty and was inconsolable.

While Tim and Capella had been in Greece, the Athens News Agency reported that Julia had tried to burn down the Mansfield house and commit suicide, only to be saved by neighbors. According to Tim the story was totally inaccurate. He said the heating had gone off in his house and Julia had lit a kerosene lamp which had started a small fire. The agency later retracted the story after Tim complained.

But in the weeks after her daughter's death, Julia Scully become increasingly hostile and bitter toward her family and Julie's friends.

"It's like a wounded animal that's just going to bite at anything around her," said Tim. "It's awful."

Finally, Tim decided it would be a good idea for his ex–mother-in-law to take Katie to visit John Junior's family in Orlando. But after a few days there Julia got in a heated argument with her son, and stormed out of the house, taking Katie.

"Tim called me up and said Julia and Katie are missing," said Tracey Allen. "She had taken Katie and disappeared."

Eventually Julia calmed down and called Tim, who

persuaded her to fly back to New York with Katie.

"We sent her to Florida and I thought everything was going to be fine," said Nist. "And then it turned into a mess."

On Saturday, February 20, Tim Nist flew back to Greece to bring Julie's remains home. Accompanying him this time was Julie's brother John, who had been granted compassionate leave by the U.S. Navy. He had taken his sister's death very badly and going to Greece became his catharsis for coming to terms with her murder.

By now the Greek authorities had formally identified Julie's body through DNA, although her head had still not been found, and may never be. Many close to Julie felt that without a head, there can be no real closure.

The day after they arrived in Greece, Tim and John Junior got a taxi to the funeral home to view Julie's remains. John went into the room where her closed casket lay to spend some time alone with his sister.

"It didn't hit home until I saw my sister's casket," said John. "Yeah, it was very emotional."

Then Tim spent a few minutes with his ex-wife's body and broke down in tears.

"I told her we had come to take her home," he said. "That's really all I said to her."

They had planned to fly to Kavala as Tim still wanted to see Skiadopoulos in jail, but the weather was so bad they had to abandon the idea. Instead they stayed in Athens, where Tim tied up some of Julie's loose ends and met the lawyers he had hired to represent the family at the upcoming murder trial.

The following Tuesday, Tim and John Junior flew back to America on a Delta Airlines flight with Julie's casket in the hold. She would finally be coming home, where she could have a decent burial.

CHAPTER TWENTY-TWO

COMING HOME

When Tim Nist brought his ex-wife's remains back to New Jersey, he felt he was finally nearing the end of a nightmare. So far his two trips to Greece and Julie's funeral expenses had cost him more than $30,000 and he had been forced to neglect his business. The memorial service was scheduled for Saturday and after that he looked forward to putting this dreadful chapter behind him and carrying on with his life.

A few weeks earlier he had asked Tracey Allen to plan Julie's funeral and she had been busy with arrangements ever since. But Julie's mother had her own ideas about what form the service should take and organized a second one for Sunday.

"I wanted to hold her service at St. Andrews Roman Catholic Church in Jobstown, where Katie was baptized," explained Tim. "Julia wanted to have it down at Immaculate where Julie was baptized."

The day after Julie's embalmed remains came back

to New Jersey, Nist went to see her black-lacquered, ornamental Greek coffin at the Peppler Funeral Home in Bordentown, and was horrified. He thought it looked like "Dracula's coffin" and found it completely unacceptable. He immediately ordered her body placed in a more American casket of natural wood.

Tracey Allen wanted the memorial service to reflect the vivacious, happy-go-lucky friend everyone had loved. She called up all Julie's friends and asked them to bring their favorite framed pictures which were put up on her casket at the funeral parlor during calling hours.

The floral arrangements were tiger lilies, which were Julie's favorite flower, and her beloved tequila shots would be served at the reception on Mansfield Road after the service.

"Choosing the verses to read at her service proved difficult for me because my pain was so great," said Tracey. "I spoke with the priest, and I expressed my wish that we focus on the fact that Julie is in Heaven now. I did not want to focus on her loss, but her gain in being with the Lord."

Realizing the memorial service would draw a lot of media, Tim planned for the camera crews and reporters to stand outside the church so they wouldn't turn it into a circus with TV lights. Print reporters would be allowed in the church during the service but all cameras would have to remain outside.

"A producer from *Extra* called," said Tim. "She wanted to put a camera in there, and I said, 'If I do it for you then I've got to do it for everyone.' In the end she never showed up because she wasn't going to get her own way."

On the morning of Julie's funeral, Tim Nist sat his

little daughter Katie down to tell her that her mother was
not coming home. He had been dreading this moment
but when it finally arrived, Katie ended up comforting
him.

"She was saying something about 'Mom,'" remembers Tim. "I said, 'Katie, come here, I've got to talk to
you about something.' I took her to my room. And I'll
never forget the look on her face when I was telling her,
'You know, your mom's not coming back. She's dead.'

"I could see by the look on her face that she kind of
knew but she was sad. I tried to explain to her about
death. 'You know, death is like—it's two parts—you
have your body and you have your soul. When you die,
your body doesn't work anymore, Your heart doesn't
work, your eyes don't work. You don't hear anymore.
It just doesn't work.

"'Your soul is when you laugh, when you cry, or
when you're happy. That's your soul and that goes on.'
So I told Katie that was part of Julie but she's not here
and you're not going to see her anymore.

"So she looked at me for a minute and she was crying
a little bit. Then she gave me a big hug and she picked
up some books and goes, 'Come on, let's go downstairs
and play.' So she actually handled it better than I did."

Later, Tim took Katie to a child analyst for a couple
of sessions to see how she was taking her mother's
death.

"She explained things to her," said Tim. "So Katie
knows the concept of the matter in the literal sense. But
she says, 'I miss my mommy.' Her mother pretty much
let her do whatever she wanted. I try and instill some
sort of discipline, as much as a father can to a daughter,
which is not an easy thing for a father to do."

*   *   *

It was a cold, blustery day as a hundred and fifty of
Julie's friends and family gathered at St. Andrews
Church to say farewell to Julie. It was a long way from
her dreams of love in a Greek paradise. For the woman
who was always desperately searching for love and felt
unloved, the service proved just how much people did
love her.

The Mayor of Trenton, Doug Palmer, attended as did
several local councilmen and other politicians who had
all been touched by Julie's story. Noticeably absent was
anyone from *The Trentonian*, with the exception of Eric
Ladley, who was covering the story for the paper. There
were also several Greek TV crews outside the church,
and Julie's service would lead off the evening news in
Greece that night.

Julie's parents both attended. It was the first time they
had seen each other since her wedding to Tim and there
was an uneasy tension between them. When Julia Scully
came into the church and saw a spray of flowers from
her ex-husband on Julie's casket, she was furious and
complained. Katie stayed at home with a baby-sitter as
Tim felt she was too young to attend her mother's funeral.

During the service Tim Nist choked back tears as he
delivered his moving eulogy to Julie, caressing a ring
that she had given him during happier times. Although
they were divorced when she died, there was no question
in anybody's mind how much he had loved her.

> When someone close to us dies, we, in our own
> minds, travel back in time with that person. We go
> to the places we've been and the people we've met
> together.
>   I would like to ask you all a question. What is

your earliest recollection of Julie? When was the
first time you met Julie? There are some of us that
have only known Julie less than a year, and there
are some of us here today that have known Julie
for more than thirty years!

When Julie was born, her mother and father
were there, time passed and her extended family
got to know her. She grew and her brother John
came along. She became a little girl with new
cousins and other kids on the street to play with.

She started school and the friendships started.
She entered high school and life-long friends came
along. Her first husband Neal was a big point in
her life, but as young love goes, it often doesn't
last. With it came new friends. Many of them are
here today.

Julie got her first job, then another. All the while
accumulating acquaintances that are still around
for her. She leaves [her teenage years] and be-
comes a young woman. It is about this time that I
came along, bringing with me new friends and new
family.

In our nearly ten years together many people
passed through our lives. For Julie there were new
careers and new adventures. We traveled, we got
married, we had a baby. Julie was my lover, my
wife, and my friend.

So you see, here today, each of us represents a
point in Julie's life.

I remember, as if it was yesterday, the first time
I met Julie. I can almost reach out and touch her.
It was at a party at the Bordentown Yacht Club on
July 8, 1989. Seven–eight, eight–nine—she always
remembered that date. She used it as a PIN number

on everything from phone cards to credit cards to combinations on her suitcases. I first saw her at a distance, and I elbowed the guy next to me, asking if he knew her.

Later that evening I saw her laughing and drinking with friends—and by the way, most of these same people are here today. Her friends got up to go into the club and she was left alone. She sat there with a cigarette hanging from her mouth, searching for a match. She had none and I sprang into action. A love affair was born!

I must tell you that when she reported to a friend about me, she said: "Well he can't be that bad, I like his dog." My dog D.J. and her are probably playing together right now.

Probably my favorite time with Julie were the early years. Being eleven years older than her, and having experienced much, it was fun to see these experiences again through young, enthusiastic eyes.

One day in 1990, on a lark, we sent in a picture of Julie to the local paper, *The Trentonian*, and Julie had a new career. This, by the way, gave Julie the opportunity to grow with confidence into the woman we all knew and loved: Our Julie!

While she continued to model, we worked together on our business. In business she was demanding and stubborn, but she was good at it. Our success was done as a team.

Then in November 1991 we married. Julie arranged the entire affair herself, and may I add paid for nearly all of it. This was Julie [all the] way through, always in control. I remember that the hall wanted to close the open bar down early. Julie would have none of that. She rushed over to the manager, wedding gown and all—well, I don't have to tell you, that bar stayed open. Julie always, somehow, got her way.

I think of how Julie was so easily liked by everyone. If there was a gathering somewhere it would be like a [fresh] blast of air [when] she entered the room, and the gathering would become a party.

All the people that know Julie now will go through the rest of our lives with questions. We now have to come to grips with the fact she's gone. You know, when someone faces death, it could be today, next week, or fifty years from now. You can't take your money, and you can't take your friends and loved ones with you. But you can take your experiences. In the end all you've got are your experiences!

I, and maybe all of you, can find solace in the fact that Julie had so many great experiences in her shortened life [and] she can carry those with her.

Julie's greatest experience was the birth of our daughter Katie. I see so much of Julie in her. I hear it in her laugh, I see it in her stubbornness, her independence, and her energy. I know they will miss each other very much. No child should be without a mother to hold her and to love her.

But Julie will manifest herself physically to Katie in many unseen ways: like the leaves that swirl around Katie in the autumn wind, this will be her mom. Or the winter snow that falls in flakes upon her head and shoulders—these will be tender kisses from her mom. In the spring when the cherry blossoms and the scent of lilac carry to Katie—

this will be her mom's perfume. And in the summer heat as the breeze whispers through the trees and cools her sweated brow—this too will be Julie, Katie's mom.

Many of us tried to pick the lock of Julie's heart. I spent the better part of ten years trying to figure out what Julie wanted, but now I know that Julie just wanted to be loved, and that's not too much to ask for, is it?

So as we go from here, all of us will have Julie in our hearts, and we [will] miss her always. Our good thoughts of her will help carry her to that better place, into God's loving arms.

When Julie and I were together, and we talked about our experiences, Julie's happiest memories were of when she was young and she camped with her family down near Cape May at a place called Dennisville Lake. Although I have never been there it seemed to leave such a lasting, happy memory for Julie.

Sometime soon her best friends and family will take Julie's [ashes] and lay her to rest near the area that she remembered so well. She'll be able to once again run through the woods, and jump the streams that roll quietly to the Delaware Bay.

She'll be able to fish and go crabbing, and it will always be summer. She'll be able to swim and go back to the camp and eat her hamburgers and hot dogs. At night when the grown-ups gather in their groups to talk, Julie will lay in her bed and listen to the music of the night.

She'll drift away to dream the dreams that little girls dream, of careers, school and friends, of traveling, having babies, and knights in shining armor. And she'll know it was all real . . .

EPILOGUE

In the months after Julie's ashes were scattered around Dennisville Lake, friends and family still found no real sense of closure. And George Skiadopoulos, awaiting his trial in Kavala Prison, remained the only one who *really* knew what he did with Julie's beautiful head.

Although he told police that he threw it into the Aegean Sea, many wonder if he didn't bury it somewhere, as his own macabre trophy of his eternal love. Now Tracey Allen and Susan White are planning to organize a search for Julie's head.

Almost all the money that Julie took to Greece has now been recovered.

On a hot, sunny July afternoon Tim Nist sat in his front room on Mansfield Road, sorting out Julie's personal possessions which had just arrived back from Greece. In the corner by the front door lay the unopened wedding dress she was to have worn when she married George Skiadopoulos. It disturbed Tim to have the dress in the house and he has asked Susan White to take it back to the shop. In the following months Tim made plans to attend the murder trial.

Now three-and-a-half years old, Katie Nist looks more like her mother than ever. She has many of Julie's traits, continually vying with her father to get her own way. Susan White and her son Robbie are regular visitors to Mansfield Road and often baby-sit when Tim is away on business.

"One night I was here watching the kids," said Sue, "and Katie said to my son, 'My mommy ran away! My mommy ran away!' And Robbie said to her, 'No, your mommy didn't run away. She loves you.' "

In the aftermath of her daughter's murder, Julia Scully moved out of Tim Nist's house and cut herself off from her family. She seldom sees her granddaughter Katie anymore and struggles through each day trying to come to grips with what has happened.

Julia says she no longer hates her daughter's murderer, refusing to waste her energy on him anymore. She now prays every day and tries to see Julie's death in the larger context of her Navajo culture.

"I was taught that the Creator already knows how long you are going to live here," says Julia tearfully. "It's all mapped out for you. Kids can die at an early age. I have to believe her death was already decided thousands of years ago before she was even born."

On Saturday, November 27, 1999, George Skiadopoulos finally went on trial, accused of killing Julie Scully and desecrating her body. Six weeks earlier a Kavala court had ruled that he could not plead insanity as a defense, ruling him legally sane when he butchered Julie. Already the high-profile murder case had been postponed for a week after Skiadopoulos's lawyer Sakis Kehagioglou, had asked for a delay, saying that he had a "problem" getting to Kavala. Now pleading guilty to Julie's murder, the former sailor faced a maximum sentence of life imprisonment without parole.

Tim Nist was in the courthouse in the tiny town of Drama, ninety miles north east of Salonika, when armed police led Skiadopoulos to the defendant's bench in chains. Now twenty-five, Skiadopoulos appeared to have been working out and had lost weight during his ten-month incarceration.

Once again Kehagioglou asked for a postponement, saying that he was still not ready to proceed, but this time presiding Judge Panayota Mandikou refused to delay the trial any longer.

During the four-day trial Tim Nist gave evidence to the three judges and four jurors through a translator, speculating that Skiadopoulos may have killed his ex-wife for her divorce settlement money. Up to that point Skiadopoulos had remained silent throughout the proceedings but now he suddenly rose from the bench.

"I have received many attacks these days," he shouted, pounding his fists on the table in front of him. "Much has been heard about financial motives but I will prove it all lies."

After he calmed down his mother Simos took the stand, blaming herself for Julie's murder. She said that growing up, her son had been "mentally scarred" by the bitter fighting between her and Pavlos Skiadopoulos during their divorce.

"Judge me, not my son," she appealed to the court, adding that she had told George that his relationship with Julie was "doomed."

"I told him that one day she will leave you," she

sobbed. "But he had blinders on. He did not understand."

A procession of character witnesses now took the stand in Skiadopoulos's defense, including his old school friend Alexis Makezedis.

On the fourth day of the trial George Skiadopoulos himself testified for five hours. He spoke mainly about his childhood and his romance with Julie, refusing to discuss the act of murder and what he had done with her head.

"I want you to imprison me," he told the judges. "I am not interested in the sentence, the prison of the soul is much worse."

Summing up, prosecutor Giorgos Siopis demanded Skiadopoulos receive the maximum sentence, declaring: "His action was the expression of evil."

During the prosecutor's closing arguments Skiadopoulos repeatedly stood up, bristling at any accusations that he deliberately murdered Julie for her money.

"Don't torture me anymore," he screamed at Siopis. "I was beyond reality when I did it. Julie was my whole life. I went crazy because I abandoned all my plans for her. I could not [handle it] when she told me we would separate. We had made so many dreams together."

On Monday, December 6—exactly a year since Julie had left Mansfield Township to move to Greece— George Skiadopoulos was found guilty of her premeditated murder and three misdemeanor counts of desecrating the dead, perjury and false testimony. The court sentenced him to the maximum of life imprisonment without parole, plus an additional five years to run concurrently on the misdemeanors. The court refused to take into account defense appeals for leniency, finding that Skiadopoulos was in a "calm and collected state" when he committed the horrific murder.

As George Skiadopoulos was led out of court through a gauntlet of Greek reporters to begin his sentence among the general population of the tough Kavala jail, his lawyer immediately lodged an appeal against the sentence.

Three days earlier Tim Nist had returned to New Jersey to look after Katie, who had been told that her father was going on a vacation.

"There are no winners with this," said Nist after hearing the sentence, which could see Skiadopoulos released in just twenty years. "I've had congratulations today, but there's a dead woman that I was married to for seven years and a little girl is without a mother now . . . It's not easy but maybe we can now move on with our lives."

NEXT STOP, MURDER...

THE RAILROAD KILLER

The Shocking True Story of Eight Gruesome
Murders and the Man Suspected of
Committing Them

WENSLEY CLARKSON

Angel Maturino Resendez is described by most who know him as
a quiet, polite, soft-spoken man, a loving husband and father to a
baby daughter. But law enforcement officials suspect that he
might be responsible for upwards of eight grisly and random
killings in a span of two years, all of which occurred near the
southwest railroad line that the killer is believed to have ridden on
his twisted murder spree. In each case, the same mode of attack—
and the same slow and painful death—appears to have been used,
pointing to the methodical slayings of a serial killer. Is Angel
Máturino Resendez the ruthless Railroad Killer—a sadistic slayer
who led police on one of the longest manhunts in history?
Bestselling true crime author Wensley Clarkson digs deep into the
heart of a horrifying murder case to uncover some stunning
answers.

AVAILABLE FROM ST. MARTIN'S PAPERBACKS
WHEREVER BOOKS ARE SOLD

TRK 3/00